To Our Readers:

INTRODUCING

OTABIND®

INTERNATIONAL

"The Book That Lies Flat"
— *User Friendly Binding* —

This title has been bound using state-of-the-art OtaBind® technology.

- The spine is 3-5 times stronger than conventional perfect binding
- The book lies open flat, regardless of the page being read
- The spine floats freely and remains crease-free even with repeated use

We are pleased to be able to bring this new technology to our customers.

Health
Communications, Inc.

3201 S.W. 15th Street
Deerfield Beach, FL 33442-8190
(305) 360-0909

OTABIND®

INTERNATIONAL

The Netherlands

SILENTLY SEDUCED

When Parents Make Their Children Partners

Understanding Covert Incest

Kenneth M. Adams, Ph.D.

Health Communications, Inc.
Deerfield Beach, Florida

Ken Adams, Ph.D.
306 S. Washington, Suite 220
Royal Oak, MI 48067

Library of Congress Cataloging-in-Publication Data

Adams, Kenneth, M.
   Silently seduced: understanding covert incest: when parents make
their children partners/by Kenneth M. Adams
      p.cm.
   Includes bibliographical references.
   ISBN 1-55874-131-3
   1. Parent and child. 2. Separation-individuation. I. Title.
HQ755.85.A32   1991
306.874—dc20   90-22950
                                                           CIP

Publisher: Health Communications, Inc.
            3201 S.W. 15th Street
            Deerfield Beach, Florida 33442-8190

DEDICATION

I dedicate this book to all
incest survivors and to the
Anonymous programs worldwide
for the hope and renewal
that they offer.

90448

ACKNOWLEDGMENTS

Many people have contributed to the creation of this book.

Steve Cross and Robin Norwood encouraged me at the beginning of this project and made helpful suggestions on the title. I am grateful to my typists, Kim Bagazinski and Nova Jeffries, for their ability to decipher my handwriting and produce the typed manuscript. Thanks to Janet Buckingham and Annabelle McIlnay for their editing which contributed to making the book more readable. I am grateful to Alec Morgan for his insight and support during times I found it most difficult to write. And I thank Susan Oddo for her enthusiasm and suggestions as I completed the final phases of the book.

I am grateful to others along the way who have contributed support and encouragement: Julie Kim Adams, Maurice Alberda, Sid Berkowitz, John Allen Bullard, Lynwood Buysse, Brent Calhoun, Lou DeCillis, Perry Engstrom, Andrea Ferenc, John Friel, Tom Garrett, Dennis Kaszeta, Earl Kilbourn, Lynne Kingsbury, Judy Norwood, Jessica Rowe, Connie Stephenson and Donny Wakefield.

Finally I would like to acknowledge the Michigan Children of Alcoholic Parents program. I am deeply indebted to the people who have journeyed through that program and shared so much of their personal struggles.

CONTENTS

PREFACE

This book grew out of an article I wrote in 1987 entitled, "Sexual Addiction and Covert Incest: Connecting the Family Roots of Alcoholism, Neglect and Abuse." At the time there had been little written on the subject of *covert* incest; most material focused on *overt* incest. Though there are certainly similarities between overt and covert incest, there are also important differences.

Although many survivors of covert incest are able to relate to the stories of overt incest survivors, most struggle to feel validated because they have not been directly abused. Covert incest survivors are still suffering in silence. In fact, most are not aware that their relationships with their parents were incestuous. I've written this book to give such survivors a framework to understand what happened to them, how their lives continue to be affected and how to begin the process of recovery.

In the first six chapters I use the word "victim" to describe the person still experiencing the effects of covert incest. These chapters describe the victimization process and its consequences. In the last chapter I discuss change and recovery. I use the word "survivor," instead of "victim," at that point to help underscore the important transformation from being a victim to re-claiming life.

This book is written primarily for the covert incest survivor who was violated by the opposite-sex parent. There are many others who have been covertly incested by the same-sex parent. Full discussion of this was beyond the scope of this book. However, the opposite-sex incest I have described parallels the damage done in same-sex incest.

The stories presented in the book are composites designed to illustrate the traits of covert incest survivors. Your actual experience may vary. No one story represents any one person's particular life. Though the stories are about heterosexual men and women, much of the material remains relevant for homosexuals as well.

To protect their right to privacy, I have purposely not used the stories of my clients. However, my thinking certainly has been influenced by their sharing. To that extent, there may be some overlap between what I have heard in my practice and what I have included in these pages. I am grateful to my clients for the sharing of their lives and the trust they have given me in the process. I respect their courage.

I hope the book becomes a part of your journey of recovery from pain and struggle to healing and freedom.

What Is The Silent Seduction?

As long as the child within is not allowed to become aware of what happened to him or her, a part of his or her emotional life will remain frozen . . . all appeals to love, solidarity and compassion will be useless.

Alice Miller
For Your Own Good

Tom came home from a long day at the office looking forward to the quiet, intimate dinner he and his wife had planned. The telephone rang. It was his mother. Now what? he thought. He listened as she described her day. Eventually she began discussing how lonely and miserable she felt with Tom's father. Tom felt his rage boil but was paralyzed by his guilt. He looked for an opening in her tirade so he could politely excuse himself and eat his dinner which was waiting for him.

1

How do I get out of this one? Tom thought, as his mother went on describing her feelings of sexual dissatisfaction with his father. Impatient and outraged, he paced the floor and hoped his mother would hang up.

When she said, "I don't know what I would do if I didn't have you. I wish your father would listen to me like you do," Tom had had enough. He hung up without a word and threw the phone to the floor in a rage. Teary-eyed, he screamed to his wife, "I don't want to know about her personal problems! I hate it, but I don't know what to do." As had happened so many times before, Tom's evening with his wife was ruined.

As a therapist I've learned Tom's story is not unique. Frequently I hear comments such as, "I can't stand it when my dad keeps telling me how much he loves his 'little princess'" or "I wish my mom would stop telling me about her loneliness. It's not my business" or "I know my dad doesn't mean anything by it, but it feels funny when he seems so worried about how I dress and gets jealous when I go out with men." The list is endless, but the theme is the same: a sense of violation and a boundary crossed. These violations are usually done in the name of "love" and "caring."

There is nothing loving or caring about a close parent-child relationship when it services the needs and feelings of the parent rather than the child. "Feeling close" with your parents, particularly the opposite-sex parent, is not the source of comfort the image suggests. It is a relationship in which the individual, both as a child and later as an adult, feels silently seduced by the parent. Feelings of appreciation and gratitude do not prevail in these "close relationships." Instead they are a source of confusing, progressive rage.

During the feedback section of my lectures on the subject, some participants are quite vocal with their rage and express relief that they now understand why at times they hate with vengeance the same parent who has always loved them "so much." Some are frozen in their seats and can't speak, while others can't wait to leave. A few courageous parents speak up, expressing that they are now beginning to understand why their sons or daughters struggle in relationships.

Others listen to the lectures and insist there is no harm in their close relationship to their opposite-sex parent. Actually they claim to feel special and privileged. These children were given a special position by being idealized by the parent. But there is no privilege in being cheated out of a childhood by being a parent's surrogate partner. As adults these individuals in turn idealize their parents to cover the pain of the abandoned and victimized child within. To be a parent's surrogate partner is to be a victim of covert incest. This book is about the silent seduction covert incest victims experience and its effect on their sexuality, intimacy and relationships.

Being a parent's surrogate partner as a child and continuing to be one as an adult has a profound effect on one's life. The following are some common characteristics resulting from the silent seduction of a covertly incestuous relationship. If you find yourself in these descriptions of characteristics, this book is for you.

1. *Love/Hate Relationship.* One often has intense feelings of both love and hate for the opposite-sex parent. On one hand you feel special and privileged because of the relationship; on the other you frequently feel you aren't doing enough for that parent. This results in feelings of guilt which result in rage that is seldom directly expressed.

2. *Emotional Distance from Same-Sex Parent.* In contrast to the love/hate relationship with the opposite-sex parent, you feel abandoned by the same-sex parent. This relationship often is competitive and the parent feels like an adversary. Feeling contempt for this parent is common.

3. *Guilt and Confusion over Personal Needs.* You feel guilty about your needs and probably have a difficult time identifying what they are. You generally try to "be strong," caretake or always "be there" for others as a way of meeting your own needs.

4. *Feelings of Inadequacy.* You are likely to have chronic feelings of inadequacy and unworthiness. You believe your

worth as a man or woman is determined by what you can do rather than who you are.

5. *Multiple Relationships.* You are likely to have been in and out of many relationships and never felt satisfied. You are always on the lookout for the perfect partner or relationship. Establishing intimacy is difficult for you.

6. *Difficulty with Commitment.* You generally experience ambivalence regarding commitment in relationships. You always seem to have one foot in and one foot out of the door just in case.

7. *Hasty Commitments.* You make a quick commitment to a relationship, then realize later it was not a good choice. You then feel too guilty to leave. Instead you try to make it right.

8. *Regret over Past Relationships.* You find yourself looking back at a previous relationship and wondering if it could have worked if you had stuck it out.

9. *Sexual Dysfunction.* You find yourself feeling sexually shut down or driven and compulsive in the pursuit of sexual highs or conquests. Sex may become addictive.

10. *Compulsions/Addictions.* You have other compulsions or addictions. You are driven in the area of work, success and achievement. You find yourself addicted to food. Either you compulsively overeat, starve yourself or you binge and purge.

When Is A Child Betrayed By A Parent's Love?

Your children . . . are the sons and daughters of Life's longing for itself. They come through you but not from you, And though they are with you yet they belong not to you.

Kahlil Gibran
The Prophet

Incest confuses and stirs us. The word is usually used to describe sexual contact between a parent and child. *Webster's New World Dictionary* defines incest as "sexual intercourse between persons too closely related to marry legally." There are both overt and covert forms of incest.

OVERT INCEST

Overt incest occurs when there is sexual contact in any dependent relationship, the most obvious being between

parent and child. However, other types of dependent relationships are experienced emotionally as parent-child due
to the nature of the interaction. These include the religious leader and parishioner, teacher and student, therapist and client or doctor and patient. Sexual contact in
these relationships often feels incestuous.

Sexual contact in dependent relationships is never jus-
tifiable because there is always a loss of choice. People in
dependent relationships seldom challenge those in positions of authority, even when they feel victimized and
violated. This is especially true when the violation is between parent and child. One of the ways parents justify
their behavior is to believe, "This is my child so I can do
what I want."

Children are not property. They feel terrified and de-
graded when a parent or any adult is sexual with them.
Cooperation does not mean they like it. They are either
too scared, too emotionally needy or too starved for affection to say no. Even if children report that at some
level they enjoyed it, the sexual contact is still emotionally
damaging. Children are generally too needy and confused
as to what is appropriate affection. Their enjoying it at
some level is a source of guilt and shame later in life. "It
was my fault because I enjoyed it and didn't say no. All my
life I carried guilt because I thought I seduced my father.
It wasn't until I went over the wreckage of my life that I
realized I was a victim of incest."

Most reports of overt incest involve girls. However,
many boys have been sexually violated by both women
and men. Unfortunately, instances of boys being violated
are under-reported. (This is changing — see Appendix for
reference to *Victims No Longer: Men Recovering from Incest
and Other Sexual Child Abuse,* by Mike Lew.) Reported cases
generally involve an adult man with a boy. However, many
boys have reported being sexually violated by their mothers, stepmothers, aunts, female neighbors and babysitters.
Sexual stereotypes about men contribute to the under-
reporting of boys who have been the victims of incest.
For example, the myth "Men are just more sexual than

women and always want sex" suggests a young boy would welcome being sexually stimulated by an adult woman. On the contrary, a young boy just learning about his body and sexuality is terrified to have a woman touch him in a sexual way.

One man described his mother's relationship with him as a child with obvious shame and confusion:

> My mother always insisted on washing my genitals, even when I was old enough to do it myself. Sometimes it was embarrassing, other times I enjoyed it. I didn't know what to think. Other times she'd give me kisses on the lips that seemed to last too long. I would often find myself sexually aroused when I looked at her. I privately felt I was strange and worried that someone would find out. To this day I feel like I was some kind of pervert because I was sexually aroused by my mother's presence.

A victim of overt incest, whether a boy or a girl, commonly reacts by internalizing fault. The victim feels responsible for what occurred. This internalization of fault or guilt inhibits healthy expression of anger. Instead, vengeance, rage and self-hatred fester. The expression of anger is necessary in the healing and *letting go* process of an incest victim.

Overt incest is one of the most frightening and traumatic experiences a young girl or boy ever has to endure. A common myth is that overt incest is the exception rather than the rule in American families. This is not the case. In his book *Victims No Longer*, Mike Lew estimates there are over 40 million American adults who as children were victims of sexual abuse. Fifteen million of them are men.

Yet, as traumatic and injurious as overt incest is, healing can occur if adults are gently guided and supported through the denial and into expression of their feelings. Victims have to be encouraged to express anger and separate from the shame and guilt. They need to be reassured that they did not cause the incest. Over time this approach helps victims to grieve the loss of their innocence regarding sexuality. Letting oneself experience the sadness and shed tears permits a cleansing of the incest experience. In its place grows a comfortableness with one's sexuality and the hope for a healthy sexual future.

Generally incest victims who do not recover are the ones who keep the experience a secret, deny it ever occurred or minimize its effect. Frequent comments include, "Well, it only happened once . . . maybe a couple of times" or "It's easier just to forget about it." As a result, the victim remains stuck in the guilt and shame. This contributes to dissatisfying intimate and sexual relationships.

Victims need support and appropriate professional guidance to recover from the violation. Incest victims (both as children and adults) may find that they report their experiences to a helping professional (therapist, doctor, clergy, nurse or teacher) and are not believed. Worse, they are sometimes accused of being the seducer. This furthers the shame and is another violation. Appropriate professional guidance which does not further the shame, is available and should be sought. Support groups such as Incest Survivors Anonymous and Survivors of Incest Anonymous are available for help. (See Appendix for listing.)

Unfortunately children are not in charge of their own destiny. When discounted by a helping professional or any adult, they fall into deep despair. Helping professionals must be willing to follow through and intervene when necessary. A helping professional who receives a report of incest and consciously chooses not to take appropriate action participates in the victimizing process. This is also true if a child goes to one parent complaining that the other is sexually abusive. For that parent to minimize or deny the violation, is to become a participant in the incest. The child is being abused by both parents through the direct sexual contact of one and the failure to protect of the other.

COVERT INCEST

Victims of covert incest, also referred to as emotional sexual abuse, suffer pain similar to that of overt victims. Identification is more difficult since direct sexual contact does not occur. However, similar feelings and dynamics are at work. (For further reading in this area, refer to *Healing The Shame That Binds You*, by John Bradshaw and *Struggle For Intimacy*, by Janet Geringer Woititz.) Although estimated numbers of overt incest victims exist, similar statistics are not available regarding covert victims. The numbers are potentially staggering, since the potential exists any time a chronic break occurs in the emotional, spiritual and sexual bond between parents.

Covert incest occurs when a child becomes the object of a parent's affection, love, passion and preoccupation. The parent, motivated by the loneliness and emptiness created by a chronically troubled marriage or relationship, makes the child a surrogate partner. The boundary between caring and incestuous love is crossed when the relationship with the child exists to meet the needs of the parent rather than those of the child. As the deterioration in the marriage progresses, the dependency on the child grows and the opposite-sex parent's response to the child becomes increasingly characterized by desperation, jealousy and a disregard for personal boundaries. The child becomes an object to be manipulated and used so the parent can avoid the pain and reality of a troubled marriage.

The child feels used and trapped, the same feelings overt incest victims experience. Attempts at play, autonomy and friendship render the child guilt-ridden and lonely, never able to feel okay about his or her needs. Over time, the child becomes preoccupied with the parent's needs and feels protective and concerned. A psychological marriage between parent and child results. The child becomes the parent's surrogate spouse.

A healthy emotional, sexual and spiritual bond between parents creates an unspoken, unseen boundary which properly channels sexual feelings and energies. When a child grows up in a family in which the marriage is chronically disturbed, sexual feelings and energy are never put into perspective and a psychological marriage with the child is formed. To the child, the parent's love feels more confining than freeing, more demanding than giving and more intrusive than nurturing. The relationship becomes

sexually energized and violating without the presence of
sexual innuendos, sexual touch or conscious sexual feelings on the part of the parent. The chronic lack of attachment in the marriage is enough to create an atmosphere
of sexualized energy that spills over to the child.

The sexual energy or tension created in a relationship
of covert incest is more akin to young love than to a
caring parent-child love. Eric described his story of growing up with an alcoholic father and a mother who kept
him close.

> My mother and I fought a lot, but I would have killed anyone who
> put their hands on her — including my father. Sometimes I had fits of
> jealous rage when she paid more attention to my father or some
> other man. She was mine and I wasn't going to share her.

Monica described her experience this way:

> I always felt special being Daddy's girl, especially when he brought
> home presents just for me and no one else. I wanted to be with him
> wherever he went. I was so in love with my daddy.

An important difference between overt and covert incest is that, while the overt victim feels abused, the covert
victim feels idealized and privileged. Yet underneath the
thin mask of feeling special and privileged rests the same
trauma of the overt victim: rage, anger, shame and guilt.
The sense of exploitation resulting from being a parent's
surrogate partner or spouse is buried behind a wall of
illusion and denial. The adult covert incest victim remains
stuck in a pattern of living aimed at keeping the special
relationship going with the opposite-sex parent. It is a
pattern of always trying to please Mommy or Daddy. In
this way the adult continues to be idealized. A privileged
and special position is maintained; the pain and suffering
of a lost childhood denied. Separation never occurs and
feelings of being trapped in the psychological marriage

deepen. This interferes with the victim's capacity for healthy intimacy and sexuality.

James' description of his divorce is a common story:

> Ann just got fed up with my putting my mother before her. We would be enjoying a Sunday, our only day off together. My mother would call and I would run right over there. I knew it was hurting my marriage, but I couldn't stand the guilt of not doing what my mother wanted. I felt trapped. Then I'd get angry with my wife and accuse her of being selfish when she complained. Finally Ann divorced me. I never understood my relationship with my mother was so damaging. It always felt good being Mom's "man of the house." My feelings for her used to be special to me, but now I only feel guilty, confused and angry.

Consider Bonnie's story. A bright, attractive professional of 40, she can't understand why she has never married, despite wanting to.

> As I started dating, I kept bringing men home for my dad to approve of, but he never did. I went through one relationship after another. I felt I would never find a man as good as my daddy. So my relationships became less and less meaningful and exclusively sexual. I became addicted to sex. When I began to need to be physically abused to be sexually aroused, I finally sought help. I had travelled far astray from my original dream of getting married to a man as good as Daddy. During therapy I learned that Daddy's special love for me actually left me feeling ashamed and angry. I had no idea being Daddy's little girl wasn't normal and set me up for a life of pain and loneliness.

These stories and similar ones are told by men and women who have been their parents' partners. The seduction inherent in these psychological marriages is subtle and insidious, as is its effect on one's capacity for a fulfilling sexual and intimate life. Since the parent-child relationship is used to meet the needs of the parent in the psychological marriage, the child feels ashamed of legitimate needs. A child seeking to have those needs met by the parent fears loss of the parent. As unhealthy as it is, the child has no choice but to actively participate in meeting the parent's needs. The child already feels emotionally abandoned, and expressing needs raises the fear of more

abandonment. Children do not have the cognitive capacity
to see the situation as it is. They are trapped.

As the children become adults, this entrapment continues
as long as the reality of being a covert incest victim continues to be denied. Adults continue to feel ashamed of
their dependency needs and seek to fulfill parents' needs at
a continued cost to their own ability to be intimate. One
important ingredient in learning to be intimate is to accept
one's own personal dependency needs. The silent seduction, if not faced directly, continues to sabotage the desire
to reap the benefits of intimacy and love with another.

THE FAMILY SYSTEM

All families function as a system in which one person's
actions affect another and vice versa. Although each member functions independently, that member also affects and
is affected by the whole. Salvador Minuchin, in *Families
And Family Therapy*, says the family system has a function
or purpose of seeking to bring itself back into balance or
stability when disrupted. So in the case of a marriage not
bonded in a healthy way, the parents' unmet dependency,
intimacy and emotional needs will be met by the rest of
the system — the children.

In a covertly incestuous relationship, the parent com-
plains to the child about the difficulties in the marriage.
The child becomes the parent's confidant. Loneliness, bitterness and dissatisfaction with the marriage and sex life
are common topics. in these discussions. The child feels
"icky" about it but quickly comes to the parent's rescue
and begins to serve as the surrogate spouse the system is
lacking. Both parents are active participants in this covertly incestuous relationship. One is getting some needs
met through the child and the other is relieved at not
having to deal with the reality of the dissatisfied partner.
Covert incest victims often report that the same-sex parent encouraged them to comfort the opposite-sex parent
after a marital fight or in their absence, for example, "You
take care of your mother while I'm gone; I'm counting on

you." The child, hoping to get some of his or her own needs met, readily obliges.

Once the boundary between parent and child is crossed in a covertly incestuous relationship, potential for more victimization exists. For example, if the oldest boy is in a psychological marriage with his mother, he may act out the covert sexualized energy with a younger sister in an overt sexual way. What started out as a spillover of unmet intimate and sexual needs from the marriage to the oldest boy in a covert way works its way into overt incest between siblings. This example clearly demonstrates how one person's behavior in a family affects the family system as a whole.

The family system works to seek balance and tries to correct itself even in adulthood. As long as the abuse or neglect experienced in childhood remains buried within, we recreate our family all over again in adult relationships. This is an effort to work out and resolve that childhood pain. Yes, the family system continues to affect one's life even when one is no longer living at home and has dismissed childhood as gone and best forgotten.

As Emily put it:

> I couldn't believe I married a man just like my father . . . at least he felt that way to me. When I married him, he seemed the opposite of my dad, but after a while we began responding to each other the way it happened with my dad. My husband began treating me like his "princess" the same way my dad did. I couldn't stand it, yet I acted in ways that demanded that kind of treatment from him. It wasn't until I was about to divorce him that my therapist helped me to see it wasn't my husband I wanted to divorce, but my past. My father.

The covertly incestuous relationship system continues to affect one's choice of partners, decisions about separation and divorce, sexuality and all attempts at emotional fulfillment until the truth is faced and resolved. This is not about blaming or accusing parents. It is about assigning responsibility where it belongs: the parents' relationship with the child. Children do not choose this relationship; it is created for them. Even as adults we do not gain

freedom of choice until we see the past clearly and experience our feelings about it. Relationships continue to be
dictated by the sense of entrapment experienced as a surrogate partner to one's parent. Assigning responsibility
where it rightfully belongs is the first crucial step in gaining access to one's true feelings, needs and wants.

I think it's important to understand that parents recreate their own family systems. Most parents are not mali-
cious and are not aware of the effect they have on their
children because a part of their own childhood is buried
within. Sadly, if one's own childhood is not seen for what
it really was, the pain of these incestuous relationships
gets passed on from one generation to the next. If parents
never recover their own lost childhoods, their grief deepens. They continue to expect their children to be there for
them in ways they hoped their parents would have been.
When this expectation goes unmet, parents see their children as ungrateful, unloving and ungiving. The result is
heightened struggles between adult children and aging
parents. Willpower or the right set of moral standards
aren't enough to produce lasting, healthy changes. Only
by facing one's past can one take responsibility for oneself
and reclaim the vitality surrendered by being a parent's
surrogate partner.

Let's take a look at two specific types of family systems
that produce a covertly incestuous relationship between a
parent and a child — the alcoholic family and the dysfunctional family.

The Alcoholic Family

Ann is a 36-year-old professional and mother of two
children. On the surface she always seemed happy and to
have everything going for her. When her marriage began
to collapse, she entered therapy and support groups for
Adult Children of Alcoholics. Ann described growing up
in her alcoholic family.

My mother was the alcoholic in my life. I was the eldest of four children and always had the duties of taking care of my brothers and sisters, the house and my dad. I resented my mother for this. But my dad praised me so much and gave me so much special attention for being the "little mother" around the house for him that eventually I didn't seem to mind my mother's alcoholism. My dad would always let me sit in his lap at night for being "his girl," comb my hair and do special things for me. Something didn't feel right about it, but it was the only attention I got.

As an adult I seemed to have everything going for me and seemed in control. But my husband confronted me one day and said he was dissatisfied with my difficulties in being intimate with him. He demanded changes or a divorce. I was stunned. That's when I discovered that growing up in an alcoholic family affected my ability to be intimate. I figured if I dealt with my feelings and issues about my mother, things would be fine. After all, she was the alcoholic. Well, I did deal with her, but things weren't fine. I came to realize all that special attention from my dad was really a source of pain and the real culprit behind my difficulty in being close to my husband.

Now that I've stopped to look, I've lived my life for him. I chose my husband because I thought my father would approve. The career and family I built were intended to win my father's admiration and love. Even as an adult I went to him with intimate details of my life, which he invited. God, I began to feel "icky" all over again. I was scared and guilt-ridden. I knew I had to stop being "Daddy's girl" if I was going to save myself and my marriage. It was the most difficult decision I ever had to make about my life, separating from the man who had been the only source of comfort while I was growing up. Yet it was also the most freeing decision I ever made.

There are an estimated 28 million children of alcoholic parents in this country, according to the National Association for Children of Alcoholics. Of that group, many have played the role of a parent's partner to fill in for the emotionally or physically absent alcoholic. These are the ones who as adults appear to have it all together and organized. They are high achieving, in control, successful and giving. They are also the ones who struggle intensely with feeling undeserving and incapable of intimacy. This pain and struggle is often hidden behind a mask of competency and proficiency in helping others. These are the children of alcoholic parents described by Sharon Wegscheider as the "heroes" and by Claudia Black as the "responsible ones."

These are roles which develop in all families during times of stress as the system tries to bring itself back into balance. In the alcoholic family the children chronically get stuck in the roles unless there is recovery of both the alcoholic and co-alcoholic (partner of the alcoholic). Alcoholism is a progressive disease process whereby the alcoholic over time becomes more and more attached to the bottle. Someone whose attachment is to the bottle cannot be emotionally attached to a partner. The vacancy created by the progressing disease makes room for a surrogate spouse. The hero or responsible child fills that space through no choice of his or her own.

The child is compelled to play the surrogate partner because it is a gratifying source of self-worth in a family with little worth to share. Again, this pattern holds true in adulthood. If the co-alcoholic is not in recovery, he or she invites and seduces a partnership with the child out of desperation to have needs met and to deny the reality of the progressing alcoholism. Alcoholic families are a true breeding ground for covert incest. Many heroes and responsible adult children have been its victims.

Heroes and responsible adult children have benefited by the recovery process offered by adult child support groups and specialized therapy programs. They have been able to let go of some of their perfectionism and feel a sense of belonging for perhaps the first time in their lives.

However, many still suffer in silence over their continued struggles with intimacy. In that silence is the "ickiness" they feel and the struggles they continue to experience with the co-alcoholic. Most fear if they talk about it at their support group meetings, they'll be ostracized by the people whose acceptance they have worked so hard for. At their meetings they do what they do best: people-please in order to be accepted. They don't talk about the truth, saying instead only what they know will be accepted. To do otherwise might "rock the boat" at their meetings. Adult children support groups sometimes have their own unspoken rules which blame the alcoholic for the pain and continue to idealize and revere the co-alcoholic for all the sacrifices offered during the adult child's growing-up years. Out of their own desperation to fill up personal emptiness, heroes or responsible adult children who have been covert incest victims perpetuate the pain by abiding by the family rule Claudia Black summarizes as *"Don't Talk, Feel Or Trust."*

One of the more difficult tasks for heroes or responsible adult children is to take themselves off the idealized and privileged pedestal they were given by the opposite-sex parent. That position represents being loved for what you can provide for your parent, not for who you are. Heroes or responsible adult children who suffered covert incest actually have been emotionally abandoned and sexually violated. Their personhood (feelings and sexuality) has been objectified or used for the purpose of another, leaving them emotionally and sexually scarred. For them, the struggle is not primarily with the alcoholic, but with the co-alcoholic.

The characteristics and patterns of the alcoholic family also hold true when a parent is addicted to drugs (including mood- or mind-altering prescription drugs), food, sex, shopping, spending, gambling or work. Like the alcoholic, the parent is emotionally absent due to the addiction. The potential for covert incest exists as a result. A chronically ill parent produces the same potential. A parent who rigidly holds on to rules dictated by a religion or ethnic tradition also becomes emotionally absent. The emotional absence occurs because the parent is more interested in upholding the moral principles of the religion or the rituals and rights of the ethnic background than in being human. The emotional life of the parent gets lost, and ultimately so does that of the marriage. This, too, produces a break in the emotional, spiritual and sexual bond of a partnership.

Covert incest is a possibility in any dysfunctional family in which there is a chronic void in the marriage relationship. Now let's take a closer look at the dysfunctional family system.

The Dysfunctional Family

Mark, a 34-year-old successful attorney, has for years had many meaningful relationships. He now finds himself lonely and destitute regarding intimacy. Mark describes his childhood.

> I thought I had the perfect parents. I was particularly fond of my mother because she was always there for me, to comfort me and talk. We talked about everything. Often she talked about my dad. I always felt special around her because she trusted me with personal information. My father was also an attorney who loved his work. He seemed more married to it than to my mother. But he made sure we had everything — the best clothes, schools and whatever we wanted. It was hard to be angry with him. Besides, as a family, we seemed fine. We were invited to all the "right" places and said and did all the "right" things. We had strong ethnic traditions and followed them to the letter. There was never any overt family fighting or feuds. We seemed real close. Yet I always found some time alone with my mother at our family gatherings. I always felt special after one of our talks.

As Mark began to face the pain of his loneliness and entered therapy, he described his family differently.

> I had no idea there were people who talked about feelings and problems directly. I was shocked to realize my family was dysfunctional. But it was true. No one ever talked about problems except when my mother complained about my dad. I never knew that in functional marriages partners spoke to each other about their dissatisfaction. I thought including me was my mom's way of making me feel special. I had no idea my mother was seducing me because she was lonely. I also began to realize my family's insistence in following tradition was an unspoken rule that said, "See, we are one big happy family and don't anyone challenge that by talking about feelings or problems directly." It was our way not to "rock the boat" and to hide all concerns. Behind that mask was the loneliness both my parents and I experienced. Since I had no knowledge as I grew up that it was okay to talk about feelings and problems, I never thought to question my mother's close relationship to me, even though at times it felt funny to be treated so special.

Mark went on to describe how his family relationships, particularly the one with his mother, affected his quest for intimacy.

I had many romantic, meaningful relationships with women. At times I was involved with more than one woman. It wasn't until I began to question my family and see the system for what it was that I realized I had ended or destroyed one relationship after another because none of the women made me feel like my mother did — her "prince" and "knight in shining armor." If I did feel 'special' in a relationship, that feeling usually didn't last long. Although there seemed to be many women interested in a "prince" to "save" them, the high or excitement with acting and being treated like one never endured. When the infatuation ended, I was faced with the realities of the person and the demands of real intimacy. So I would drop or destroy the relationship in search of the woman who would make me feel special forever. Of course this never happened, and I became more lonely than I imagined I could be. I was desperate. I never dreamed this was the result of my family system. This awareness was both enraging and freeing.

Many men and women have grown up in families where there is no alcoholic or chemically dependent parent, yet the struggles for love and intimacy are similar. In fact, many of these families appear well put together, almost the ideal or perfect family on the outside. This makes it much more difficult to confront the past in an effort to find the roots of one's current struggles to grow and become healthy. These dysfunctional families have been described as co-dependent. In *Co-Dependency And Family Rules: A Paradoxical Dependency*, Robert Subby and John Friel offer this definition:

Co-dependency is a dysfunctional pattern of living and problem-solving which is kept in place by a set of rules within the family system. These rules make healthy growth and change very difficult.

These rules are described by Subby and Friel as follows:

1. It's not okay to talk about problems.
2. Feelings should not be expressed openly.
3. Communication is best if indirect, with one person acting as messenger between two others (triangulation).
4. Be strong, good, right, perfect. Make us proud. (Unrealistic expectations.)

5. Don't be "selfish."
6. Do as I say, not as I do.
7. It is not okay to play or be playful.
8. Don't rock the boat.

These rules, practiced collectively or singly, make it difficult for people to be close or intimate. The desire to share oneself (i.e., feelings, thoughts, preferences, wants and needs) becomes frightening. The family system's mask of perfection and idealism is threatened. These families, with their codes of silence, suffer from chronic tension and anxiety that lurk below the surface. Remarks such as, "You could have cut the tension with a knife," are not uncommon. Family members operating in these systems are usually relieved no one said anything, for fear of what might happen — "I'm sure glad I got out of there before someone said something."

Talking about feelings or problems helps to resolve tension. These families believe, however, that if they don't talk about problems, the tension will go away. Any sort of emotional bonding between family members is impossible as long as these rules are observed.

Although there is no clearly absent parent due to alcohol or drug abuse, families operating under co-dependent rules create the potential for a covertly incestuous relationship. Co-dependent families originate from marriages which operate in a code of silence. Even though there is no obvious break, healthy intimacy and sexuality have no chance to grow. One or both partners will feel dissatisfied.

Trapped by a set of rules which do not permit the healthy expression of feelings and problems, a parent can easily turn to a child to get needs met. This child lessens the parent's loneliness and helps the parent deny the breakdown inherent in a marriage built on co-dependent rules. It is easy to see how a parent can channel his or her passion and energy into the child and how that child can feel like the parent's surrogate partner. For the adult child of a dysfunctional family, the task of seeing the family for what it is becomes difficult due to the family's rigid adherence to the idealistic or perfect image. To name the covert incest that went on is much more difficult. Yet to break the walls of silence and denial is far better than to keep the pain and suffering of being a parent's surrogate partner secret for a lifetime.

The Man Of The House

Early on we experience women as the ones who fill us up, who comfort and take care of us, without an opportunity in growing up . . . to feel truly separate from women.

Samuel Osherson
Finding Our Father

MOM'S LITTLE MAN

When Ed entered therapy, he was forlorn with an air about him that said, "Don't try to help me. I can do it myself." Serious in expression and rigid in manner, he answered questions more like a good soldier than someone seeking help. He wasn't sure why he was in a therapist's office except he had felt depressed for too long and couldn't get rid of this feeling. After many sessions Ed finally became more comfortable and began to loosen up.

In an almost proud and boastful manner he described
his childhood.

> I was seven when my dad left the house. I really never knew why,
> and I don't have a lot of memories before that age. I only knew I was
> the eldest in a family of eight, and it just seemed like I was the new
> dad. In fact, I can still remember my mother's words the day after my
> dad left: "Your father won't be coming back, and you're going to have
> to help me with the kids." It was a moment of both delight to be Mom's
> helper and confusion as to what happened to my dad. When I tried
> to clear up my confusion by asking my mother what happened to
> Dad, I was usually met with short angry comments about what a "no
> good" man my father was. To this day, I still don't understand why he
> left. What I do know is that the sadness I felt about my dad leaving
> was quickly replaced by anger nurtured continually by my mother. I
> decided early on I was going to show him I could be a better father
> than he ever was. Although I didn't know it at the time, I was also
> working on being a better husband than he was — a role my mother
> always seemed to welcome.
>
> I took on my role dutifully and became more like a drill sergeant
> than a brother to my brothers and sisters. I made sure they did their
> homework, cleaned their rooms and listened to Mom. When they
> wouldn't listen to me, I'd yell and scream and sometimes hit them.
> Once I spanked my younger sister for not washing the dishes. They
> all hated me, but at the time it didn't seem to matter. Because Mom
> always supported my disciplining the kids, I felt powerful and deserv-
> ing. I also began doing odd jobs in the neighborhood and got a paper
> route so I could help Mom support the family. I was serious and
> dependable, so I readily got jobs that were meant for someone older.
> By the time I was eleven I was handing out allowances to each of my
> brothers and sisters. In school I always felt distracted by my respon-
> sibilities at home and never had time to play or join extracurricular
> activities. By the time I was twelve I was a grown man who had never
> known the meaning of play and fun.

It is clear Ed had lost his childhood long ago and had
become the "man of the house" in a family desperate for
structure and direction. His teen years continued the
pattern.

> More and more, my mother and I stayed up late talking. I loved our
> talks. She would tell me about her day and how glad she was I was
> home waiting for her. Sometimes she cried about how lonely she was
> and leaned against me on the couch until she fell asleep. I would

cover her up and kiss her good night before going to bed myself. There were moments when I wished I could have slept with her. Although those feelings alarmed me, I felt too ashamed to say anything to anyone. Besides, there was no one in my life I could talk to except my mother.

One Christmas I decided I was going to make my mother feel special so she wouldn't have to feel so lonely. I went out and bought her expensive perfume, a special nightgown, and a fancy necklace. She loved the gifts and seemed to love me more. She held me close while we watched everyone else open their presents. That night she kissed me good night and told me I was her "little man." It felt great being treated so special. It gave me a feeling of power.

It wasn't until I started dating and bringing home girlfriends that I began to feel anger toward my mother. Actually I became enraged. At first it seemed nice to be able to come home and talk to Mom about my dates, but then she began to get jealous. In fact, when I became serious about Susan, my mother forbade me to see her and accused her of being a slut. I stormed out of the house and made my way to Susan's house. By the time I got there my rage was covered over by a sense of guilt that permeated every cell of my body. To my surprise I broke off my relationship with Susan and went home like a puppy with his tail between his legs. I was still angry, and I felt trapped.

Finally, when I was 24, I left home to marry Karen. Karen was a nice girl. My mother didn't seem too threatened by her and reluctantly approved of her. It seemed like a juggling act to attempt to get my needs met and not feel guilty at the same time. Shortly after I married, I became engrossed in my work. I was powerful, competent and successful on the outside but I felt impotent and angry on the inside. My marriage lacked vitality and passion. I felt as trapped in my marriage as I did in my relationship with my mother because she always made her presence known in my life. At work I began to find myself more and more angry at female subordinates, eventually being seen as a chauvinist. At other times I found myself acting seductively with these women and contemplating affairs.

When I failed to get a promotion because of my attitude problems at work, my world seemed to fall apart. I became more and more depressed. Inside I was screaming, "Help, this is not who I am!" Yet I had no idea who I was. Guilty, confused and angry, I finally sought help.

Ed's story is like those of many men who spent their childhoods being "the man of the house." Men like Ed are blamed for not being emotionally available for intimacy because of workaholism and chauvinistic attitudes. These are just symptoms of a root pain and suffering hidden behind an arrogant, boastful facade. These men are lacking an emotionally fulfilled and sensitive identity because of repeated violations of their personal boundaries by their mothers.

Due to their shame and confusion, men like Ed bury their rage and hurt early on through denial. Everything buried in childhood finds its way out through one's personality and behavior patterns. It is no surprise that there are so many angry, arrogant men struggling intensely with feelings and intimacy.

Ed's wife, Karen, had her own difficulties with intimacy. Behind the image of being "nice" was someone terrified of herself and intimacy. Being nice was the only way Karen knew to express her love. Attempts at passion, joy or healthy conflict were generally suppressed. Ed's marriage to Karen was more his mother's choice than his own. In addition Ed needed to choose someone who herself had struggles with intimacy so the marriage would not become fulfilling. For if it did, it would feel like an affair. Ed's primary partner was still his mother. Karen became the "other woman." Ed's depression resulted from both the insidious spiritual deadening of his marriage and long-term grief over a lost childhood.

If Ed is to recover his potential for emotional fulfillment and intimacy, he has to face the pain and anger of being his mother's partner. To deal only with the surface issues of workaholism and attitude problems will not produce any lasting change.

For Ed and Karen's marriage to become fulfilling requires a change in Karen as well. Once Ed begins to separate from his mother, he will experience the marriage differently. While it was once a source of pride and comfort to have married a "nice girl," it is now a source of anger and resentment. Ed will begin to experience Karen's own difficulties with being close and desire someone able to be intimate. It was no accident, either, that Karen chose Ed to marry. Karen's own childhood of abuse or neglect would have compelled her to marry someone like Ed.

MAMA'S BOY

Yeah, I was mama's boy all right. We were best friends, I suppose. I know I was sure special to her. She took me everywhere with her: shopping, lunch with her friends and sometimes even to bed when my dad went out of town on business. It seemed she always treated me as her "little baby" even as I grew up. She protected me from my brothers when they tried to start a fight. My mom would keep me home from school even when I wasn't sick. She said she needed some company, and I could make up my schoolwork later. I never did. I was either at home with my mom, out sick or distracted from my schoolwork because I was worried about mom. School was a struggle, and I was called names like "sissy" and "baby." My brothers called me names, too, and hated that I was so special to my mom.

This was Tom's initial response when asked what his childhood relationship with his mother was like.

Tom entered therapy reluctantly and only because he had become sexually compulsive with prostitutes. He had a history of compulsive masturbation and use of pornography to get sexually high. Recently, however, it didn't seem to be working. He vowed he would never visit prostitutes, but found he couldn't stop himself. Having sex with prostitutes was more taboo and produced the high he was after. He was confused and scared.

Tom continued to describe growing up in his family.

I was the youngest of four children, which seemed to contribute to being "mama's boy." In looking back, I guess my mother and father never had a very good relationship. My dad was an alcoholic and my mother was very religious. They always bickered. They seldom slept together and when they did, I was often between them. I was the one who got the good morning kiss when we got up, not my dad. Although it seemed a little funny, I liked being treated so special.

My mom pampered me all my life. Anything I wanted, I got. I became oblivious to my brothers and sister and, basically, the world at large. All that seemed to matter was being with my mother. I felt as if my dad hated me. It seemed to me he was actually jealous. Even today my father mumbles under his breath that it was my fault they got divorced.

I still remember the scene when my mom kicked my dad out. She held me in front of her with her arm around me as she told him she was tired of his drinking and wanted him out. My father yelled back at her that he wouldn't drink so much if she paid half as much attention to him as she did to that "damn kid," pointing at me. He slammed the door. I remember feeling terrified and confused as to why my dad was so angry at me. The next morning he came back, packed his things and left. It was confusing to me that I didn't even miss him. I didn't know him. My mother had kept me close to her for so long I didn't know what it was like to have a father.

I didn't date too much in high school, mostly because I felt guilty leaving my mom. I did, however, begin a secret life of masturbating to pictures of women in magazines and eventually to pornography. I didn't know exactly what was going on but it relieved me. I started feeling resentful that she wanted me so close. The masturbation seemed to help me deal with my feelings.

I'm not sure what propelled me, but I decided I had to leave the house. So at the age of 25 I left. It was so difficult — my mother was enraged and I felt terrible guilt. I had to get out. Besides secretly I had started seeing women. I didn't want to tell my mom because I didn't think she would understand. I also was masturbating more, to the point where I couldn't live without it.

I discovered if I played the aimless, cute, little-boy role I learned from my mom, women would "come on" to me. They wanted to take care of me like my mom did. It was an easy way to get sex. I became obsessed with sex and never was able to have a serious or intimate relationship. My mother and I continued to talk often, even though I didn't live with her anymore. She thought it would be a good idea if we spent more time together, so I began to spend some of my weekends with her. I think it was at this point that the compulsive masturbation wasn't enough. Frequently after a weekend with my mother, I sought sex with prostitutes.

God, I really began to feel confused. Even though I didn't want to admit it, my special relationship with my mom was a source of pain and personal invasion. I began to feel angry with her, but I didn't want to let go of the special attention I was getting. It seemed like I couldn't live without my mother.

Tom's story is one of a sexual addict, someone whose life is unmanageable due to the compulsive pursuit of sexual highs. (There will be a more thorough discussion of sexual addiction in Chapter Five.) Tom's story reflects the escalation or tolerance in sexual pursuits which is characteristic of sexual addiction. Being sexual with prostitutes represented a violation of his personal value system. The covert incestuous relationship with his mother was a major factor in his sexual compulsiveness. The fact that the escalation of his addiction began after he went back to spend the weekends with his mother suggests that his rage at being seduced had festered. Being obsessed with sex was the way Tom distracted himself from the pain of the covert incest.

Due to the perceived entrapment from his guilt, Tom found it difficult to accept his rage as legitimate. However, all feelings find their way out in spite of one's suppression of them. In Tom's case, his sexual addiction was an expression of his rage and shame. His manipulation to have sex with women represents an attitude of exploitation of them. His treatment of women as objects to "get" and "use" was the relief valve the rage needed. As his mother's seduction increased, so did Tom's rage.

Also noteworthy in Tom's story is the competition set up between him and his father. The seduction by his mother pitted Tom against his father. Tom's father naturally felt jealous and competitive toward him. This competition is a frequent dynamic in covert incest, with the same-sex parent usually looking like the "bad guy." Tom's father felt pushed out, which may have been part of his mother's motive (probably unconsciously). The legitimate anger existing for Tom toward his father was because his father was unwilling to step in and separate Tom from his mother. Tom's father either perceived the covertly incestuous relationship as too powerful to break into or was relieved by it since it gave him an excuse to leave the relationship with his wife.

Even if the dynamics and feelings are completely understood, therapy is not enough for a sexual addict. Sexual addiction, like all addictions, does not readily respond to advice, logical arguments, insight or awareness. A recovery process similar to the one used in the treatment of alcoholism is required to stop compulsive sexual behavior. Alcoholics Anonymous is the recovery program used by alcoholics. There are separate Anonymous programs which exist for sexual addiction: Sex Addicts Anonymous, Sexaholics Anonymous and Sex and Love Addicts Anonymous.

THE PRINCE

Handsome, charming, and seemingly able to "talk a good game," Jeffrey began discussing why he wanted to be in therapy.

I was shocked when I discovered through the grapevine at work that because I wasn't married, I didn't get the promotion I was after. I didn't fit the company image. I worked toward this position for a long time and counted on it. My qualifications were outstanding. What did my personal life have to do with the job? Initially I was angry and thought about contacting my attorney. However, after finding myself sobbing at home that evening, I thought better of it. I couldn't remember myself ever crying before, not even as a kid except when I wanted my way. I knew something was wrong.

I never questioned my insatiable appetite for the company of women. I never seemed satisfied with dating just one woman. I always had to be involved simultaneously with many. For the most part, I was usually honest about dating around, so I never gave it a second thought. Besides women seemed more than willing to compete. I loved the attention. It made me feel like a king. Dating became more like a sport than an attempt at developing a relationship. During the times I was dating just one woman, it was never enough. I had to have more. I generally didn't spend more than one or two days in a row with any one woman, thinking I wanted to be careful not to get too tied down. Yet if I wasn't seeing someone on a given day I was planning my next encounter. My life became consumed with the pursuit of women. I suspect the reason I didn't get my promotion was more involved than just not being married. I wonder if the reputation I had as a lady's man was what really interfered.

When any woman I was dating began to make demands of my time or wanted a commitment, I stopped seeing her. Shortly after I began looking for a replacement. I usually felt panicky and desperate until I filled the space left by her departure. During those rare times when I had a long-term girlfriend, I felt suffocated and never remained faithful. In my twenties it was, "I'm too young for a commitment." In my thirties it was, "I have some time left." Now at the age of 47 I find myself saying, "I'm not the marrying type." Privately I've been waiting for the perfect woman. I realized for the first time just how lonely and fearful I really am. It seems I've spent the better part of my life running from something though I can't see what it is.

Jeffrey had a difficult time relating to a male therapist. Men like Jeffrey usually relate to other men by bragging about their escapades and discussing women as they discuss the attainment of a sports trophy. Sharing intimately is frightening and avoided at any cost. With women Jeffrey was likely to brag about himself, embellish stories and talk "intimately" only as a means to seduce. Relationships with both men and women leave men like Jeffrey feeling alone and empty. Over time Jeffrey developed enough trust to begin identifying what he was running from.

I never imagined my childhood had much to do with the struggles I was experiencing with women and intimacy. My family was always a place where I was treated like a prince, especially by my mom. I had an older sister who was "my dad's" and I was "my mother's," creating what seemed like a division of loyalty. My mom was always on my side anytime there was conflict. She always indulged me. Anything I wanted, I got. She was at my beck and call. She showered me with gifts, fussed over me and told me how handsome I was. She would tell me, "Someday you will be a lady's man."

She was always preoccupied with my appearance and not uncommonly talked about my body. I remember once as a teenager she actually made a comment about how good I looked in tight jeans. I felt embarrassed and a little funny but never thought anything of it. Already as a teenager, I seemed to be attractive to girls. It felt great. At school I got lots of attention from my girlfriends, and at home I got even more from my mom. I see now that as early as then, I couldn't get enough attention from girls.

My mother actually encouraged me to go out with girls and she never put any restrictions on the time I had to be home. Once I stayed out all night. When I got home in the morning, my mom just gave me a big smile and kiss saying she "knew what I was doing." I just smiled back until my father came into the room. He gave me a vicious look and wanted to know where the hell I had been all night. My mother immediately came to my defense and told him I was just being a boy. As she left for work she reminded me, as she frequently did, that I shouldn't get too attached to any one girl so I could "shop around" for the perfect one.

There was mostly distance between my father and me. He never seemed to have much time for me and spent a great deal of time away from the house. He worked a lot, and sometimes I wondered if he had another woman on the side. My dad never got drunk or physically abused me. He just wasn't there. I never could figure out why my parents stayed together. They were both working professionals and, on the surface, seemed not to have time for each other. But it went deeper than that. Even when they were together, they didn't talk

to each other much. They really were unhappy together. I see now
why my mother invested so much energy in me.

The relationship Jeffrey's mother had with him was
sexually energized. Jeffrey probably felt stimulated early
in childhood by his mother's intense passion toward him.
Certainly his tale of his mother's apparent pleasure in
knowing he had spent the night with a girl strongly suggests she was vicariously enjoying a fantasy of her own.
Confused and with no one to talk to, Jeffrey suppressed
feelings of shame and anger at being violated. Further, he
would have had to deny that his mother's treatment of
him felt invasive and to continue believing he was her
"prince." Over time his feelings of shame and anger buried
deeply within evolved into contempt and rage toward all
women. Playing the "lady's man" was a mask for this contempt and rage and a way to act those feelings out.

Psychologically it is generally believed a "lady's man" or
"womanizer" is really trying to gain control or power
over women. Certainly this is true. In extreme cases
hatred and abuse of women develop. However, at a deeper level the "lady's man" avoids the pain of being violated
by his mother and acts out his rage specifically about her
as opposed to women in general. As time goes on, such a
man has to date more, hate more or abuse more to sustain the denial of feelings about the incest with his mother. In Jeffrey's case, the desperation and panic he felt
when he wasn't seeing someone suggested his suppressed
feelings were trying to find their way to the surface.
Being denied the promotion at work was the catalyst
which broke down Jeffrey's defenses and left him with
the pain of the trauma of being seduced by his mother
and abandoned by his father.

Also at issue here, at least on the surface, is Jeffrey's
fear of intimacy. This expression gets tossed around a lot
these days, particularly when discussing men. Certainly
Jeffrey's inability to make a commitment qualifies him as
someone who fears intimacy. Yet just to work at finding
ways to help him become more intimate is not the remedy.

It is not so much the fear of intimacy that is operating here, but the fear of feelings a commitment would bring to the surface. A committed relationship would re-engage the original emotional-intimate system (Jeffrey's family) he carried with him into adulthood. In that committed relationship, all those feelings and issues still unresolved would surface so he could finally work them through and feel at peace within himself. It's the psyche's way of healing old emotional wounds.

Without the proper context of understanding and the means to alter one's behavior, the pain of the original trauma continues and the old patterns keep repeating themselves. In Jeffrey's case, he seduced and objectified women as his mother did to him in their covertly incestuous relationship. Given the intense passion and sexual preoccupation Jeffrey's mother had toward him, it is likely that she was herself an incest victim acting out with Jeffrey what had been done to her. Incest victims may choose partners who have difficulty with sexual boundaries in an effort to work out the shame and anger. This suggests Jeffrey's suspicion of his father having extramarital affairs was probably accurate. In turn Jeffrey's parents were re-enacting scenes from their own childhoods. Jeffrey was the next victim in line for the spillover of inappropriate sexual energy transmitted over generations of victims.

One final note regarding Jeffrey's case: He, like many men who have reputations as "womanizers," was primarily interested in the sexual conquest of women. This type of pattern reflects sexual addiction. Jeffrey was able to face this and begin participating in an Anonymous program for sex addicts. As a result, he was finally able to face the feelings he had been running from for years. In time he developed a sense of hope and contentment.

MOM'S CONFIDANT AND ADVISOR

When Peter came for therapy, he complained of feeling burned out and lethargic. He was a successful therapist who, in spite of his thorough understanding of himself, was unable to stop overcommitting and overextending himself. His life primarily consisted of helping, pleasing and being there for others. He complained of having no sense of identity and not having any free time for himself. Peter felt unappreciated and that others took advantage of him. He reluctantly acknowledged that for some time he had resented his wife. He complained he was always there to listen to the multitude of problems she had, but he never felt he got equal time. Yet Peter claimed to be going out of his way to be there for his wife even more than he had done previously. He felt crazy. He was sexually shut down and had lost all interest in being intimate with his wife.

Relieved to have someone listen, Peter talked rapidly and obsessively, trying to get his whole life story out in one therapy session. His initial focus was his wife.

I first met Susan ten years ago when she was trying to break up with her then current boyfriend. She was very troubled and needed someone to talk to. I was more than happy to be there for her. I saw it as a way to get her to like me. I knew I could be good to her and could help her change.

Our initial dates basically consisted of me listening and Susan talking about how much her boyfriend had hurt her. I offered support and plenty of advice as to how she should handle the situation. She often showed up at my apartment after seeing him, crying and confused. Even our beginnings at being affectionate were me holding her while she cried about her boyfriend. The first time we made love was after she cried in my arms about him. Privately I wondered who she was really making love to. It was months before she stopped seeing her boyfriend, and that was only because he insisted they no longer see each other.

Even after that Susan seemed preoccupied with him. However, I didn't spend much time considering my feelings about the situation because I was so involved with being her "counselor." Eventually she seemed to forget him, and we got married. Our marriage continued to consist of me being preoccupied with how she was feeling and adjusting my schedule to meet her needs. I was driven in my efforts to be there for her, believing she would stop wanting me if I wasn't helping her in some way.

At first she seemed to crave the attention as much as I was obsessed in giving it. But over time we seemed to grow more distant. Susan no longer seemed to appreciate my efforts to be there for her,

and I began to resent her. And my obsession to help only increased.
I felt drained and empty. I resented that I knew I wasn't going to be
able to count on Susan to be there for me. She also claimed to have
lost respect for me because I was always trying to help her. Yet my
efforts to manage her life and problems escalated.

I was having similar problems at work. I was unable to set limits on
the amount of time I was available for clients and had a difficult time
collecting fees. I began to resent the work I loved so much. My
friendships were based primarily on me "being there for" or "helping"
my friends. I resented that no one seemed to care about my problems. I was so desperate to be liked I never let on to anyone that I had
personal problems or personal needs. I did what I knew best in order
to secure friendships: helping others out. Naturally, I chose as friends
those people whose lives were troubled. I have become so resentful
I could explode, except I feel too depressed to do so.

Peter's story is not unlike those of other helping professionals: doctors, therapists, ministers or nurses. On
the outside is a mask of competence supported by a proficiency in helping others. Underneath the mask are feelings of neglect, resentment, bitterness and fear. Needs
are met through manipulation of others by always being
there for them. These individuals gain their self-esteem
through pleasing and helping others. But this sense of
esteem is false. Feelings of worthlessness and shame generally prevail underneath the exterior of "being so together."
A compulsion and desperation to help others usually consumes the lives of individuals like Peter. They hope that
soon they will feel worthy and have their own needs met.
This never happens and the desperation grows.

A closer look at Peter's childhood reveals the origins of
the emotional trap in which he finds himself ensnared.
Peter was the younger of two children, with an older
sister. His parents were both successful professionals who
always presented a good image to those outside the family.
However, his parents had chronic problems in their marriage. His father worked a lot. When he was home, he was
often moody. Peter's mother was particularly dissatisfied
and bitterly complained about her husband to Peter. Peter,
being the "sensitive one" in the family, was always willing
to listen.

Peter described his relationship with his mother and father.

> I always seemed to be in the middle of the two of them. My mother complained she wasn't getting enough attention and affection from my father. I would tell my dad about it and encourage him to pay more attention to her. He seldom did, and I began to resent him. I then went to my mom to console her. She would go on and on about my father. I would offer advice and counsel my mother so she would feel better.
>
> I remember that as young as eight years old, I was telling my mother she didn't have to worry about my dad because she had me and I loved her. I still remember the big smile when I told her "I love you." She hugged me and held me close. It felt so good to be able to make my mom stop crying and put a smile on her face. I was more than willing to be there for her. I felt so important and powerful. I continued to tell my father about how upset mom was in hopes that he would change. But he never did, and I was the one who was there for my mother.
>
> This pattern continued throughout my childhood and adolescence. After a while it seemed that my mother actually preferred my company over my father's. She basically stopped complaining to him directly about how unhappy she was. Instead, she talked to me about it. I remember she would call me into her room after work to talk while she changed clothes. Although she never actually took all of her clothes off in front of me, she would take off her jewelry and shoes, and unzip before she asked me to leave. After dinner she would ask me to help her around the house. She would talk about her day at work and her problems with my dad. Sometimes it felt funny being so close to Mom, but it was such a feeling of importance that it didn't seem to matter.
>
> Even as an adult, I still feel caught between my mom and dad. I'm the messenger. When Mom is unhappy, she calls me to complain and then puts Dad on the phone. I can't believe I still do this. It enrages me, but I feel guilty thinking about setting limits on my mother. After all, she is the one who cared about me so much when I was growing up.

Peter's last statement reflects the essence of his adult struggles. He came to believe his mother's relationship with him was a statement of her love for him. It may be true that Peter's mother loved him, but her need to have him around her so much was to service her own needs, not his. Her behavior was not a statement of love for him but of need for him. As a result, Peter's own needs for love, security and support were never met. His relationship with his mother became a model or prototype of how he would seek out love in his adult life. It is not surprising Peter married Susan, a woman who required a great deal of caretaking and was unable to care for him in return.

The covert incest occurred as a result of the role in which Peter played the surrogate husband. Counseling his mother about the unhappiness in her marriage was not his responsibility, nor was reassuring her that she was loved. That discussion needed to occur between husband and wife. Sexual energy was certainly felt when he was invited into her room after work. His mother's own neediness prevented her from realizing that her behavior was inappropriate.

Peter's situation did not result in a sexual addiction but rather a sexual shutdown. Denying his sexual expression was a way Peter could remain loyal to his mother. His passion was still his mother's, not his. Circumstances like Peter's could result in sexual addiction or other addictions for that matter — relationship, alcohol, drug or food. For Peter, work could certainly be considered addictive and a re-enactment of the role he played in his family.

Men like Peter search for women they can take care of. It's almost magnetic. The hope is, "If I can just be there enough for her, maybe she'll be there for me." Generally that never happens. Instead the needs remain unmet and the resentment grows. For the most part, however, the needs Peter longs to have met cannot really be fulfilled by his wife. They are needs of childhood which are more appropriately met through support groups and the therapy process. That is not to say there aren't legitimate needs that were not being met in Peter's marriage. The emotional bind he was in was a result of his position between his mother and father.

Peter acted as a messenger between Mom and Dad. This is another area of his childhood in which he was exposed to inappropriate sexual energy. Being the messenger between his parents regarding their intimacy issues left Peter exposed to a passionate energy meant to be exchanged between husband and wife. This was the factor behind Peter's becoming so involved with Susan while she was breaking up with her boyfriend. Symbolically Susan was his mother; her boyfriend was Peter's father. Peter essentially has re-enacted his unresolved childhood pain through Susan by recreating what happened to him as a child. Peter's choice of careers in the helping profession and his difficulty setting limits is also a reflection of the bind he was placed in as a child.

For Peter to resolve the issues surrounding his marriage and career requires addressing the covert incest with his mother and the abandonment by his father. Trying to resolve his current adult issues by focusing only on the present is like trying to plug a hole in a dam with one finger while other holes keep breaking through. It is the reservoir of feelings, backed up over a lifetime, that must be addressed. Peter needs to resolve his rage, bitterness and guilt about the role he was placed in during childhood, a role which extended to his adult life. This requires grieving for his lost childhood and the fact that his needs were not met. This grief is the root cause of his depression.

THE VICTIMIZING PROCESS

Peter and the other three men presented in this chapter are not unique. Their stories are common to men who have grown up in alcoholic or dysfunctional families. But covert incest is not limited to the four roles identified in this chapter. Boys playing roles such as the family's or Mom's hero, Mom's lover boy or golden boy are also potential victims of covert incest. The covert incest they suffered has been a source of confusing, progressive rage and shame that has plagued their intimate and sexual lives as adults. Identifying this victimizing process is the first step necessary in getting free of the trap of being a surrogate partner. Although there are a myriad of issues regarding intimacy for these men, the dynamic of being a covert incest victim is most pervasive.

A few other issues warrant addressing before we move on to stories of women who were their fathers' partners. The first, a common reaction of many when hearing this information about being a covert incest victim, is, "If it weren't for my mother, nobody would have cared about me. My dad didn't seem to care about me, and I felt abandoned by him. So even though my mom seemed a little overbearing and overprotective, at least she cared about my needs."

First, it is true that these men have been abandoned by their fathers and this experience is both highly significant and damaging. One's sense of manhood is deeply injured. To capture a vital and healthy sense of being a man requires dealing with the anger and sadness of the abandonment. It also requires that these men, in adulthood, begin replacing the loss which occurred as a result of being abandoned. This process will be discussed more fully in the final chapter.

The reality about being abandoned by the father is clear. It is not confusing, and the feelings are readily accessible if one has the necessary support. However, the reality of a mother's behavior toward a child in a covertly incestuous relationship is not clear. There is a grave distortion in perception. It isn't always the abuse, neglect or abandonment one suffers as a child which later interfere with happiness, but rather the distortion in perception which results. The classic example is, "I beat you for your own good." Certainly being beaten is damaging, but being told it is for one's "own good" is the factor that will haunt the child for a lifetime.

Being a covert incest victim is no different. It is a distortion in perception to believe that the mother's excess attention given in a covertly incestuous relationship saved the child. On the contrary, it robbed the child of the freedom to be autonomous and to feel worthy. Vitality is lost under the insidious, life-long trap that "I should keep being there for my mother; after all, she was always there for me." Again it cannot be stressed enough that the mother's preoccupation with the child is not a statement of love for the child, but a statement of dire neediness by the mother. The child's core needs are not served but rejected. The child feels like an object, not a person. The real needs for love, nurturing, security and trust are never met. Worse yet, the child is made to believe they are met. This is the essence of the damage in a covertly incestuous relationship, along with the trauma of that relationship being bound by inappropriate sexual energy. The reality here is not clear. That is a major factor in covert incest being so insidious and pervasive in an adult victim's life.

If you are a man and find yourself identifying with being a covert incest victim, it would be good to keep in mind that the intent here is not to blame your mother but to hold her accountable. It is also important to keep in mind that your mother's behavior was largely unconscious. Even if it had been conscious, her own neediness from her damaged childhood would have prevented her from taking more personal responsibility. To continue to deny the damage the relationship has caused will keep you trapped in the struggle to find contentment with yourself and your partner. To focus only on your anger about your father's abandonment keeps the denial alive.

The final commentary about this victimizing process refers to the fact that it is a set-up for some form of addictive or compulsive lifestyle. Because of the broken spirit, pain and discomfort of being objectified as a child and feeling inappropriate sexual energy, the adult covert incest victim has a difficult time being comfortable with his body. Addictions represent an escape from the body and a way to medicate feelings. Sexual addiction and workaholism have already been mentioned in some of the stories. However, food addiction, alcoholism, compulsive spending, shopping, gambling and drug addiction are also common. The list is endless. One can become addicted to anything. Surrendering or letting go of the addiction is the first order of business in being able to identify and stay with the feelings of being a covert incest victim.

4

Daddy's Little Girl

*When my daddy died, it seemed like I lost the love of my life.
I was so in love with him . . . I can't seem to love anyone like
I loved my daddy.*

Anonymous

During the industrial revolution, fathers began to be absent from the home in numbers unmatched at any previous time in history. Often one of the sons was left in charge while the father worked and subsequently became vulnerable to becoming his mother's surrogate spouse. This socio-cultural factor has left more men than women victims of covert incest. Yet women also fall victim to this seduction. And for women there are additional complications not as common for men. For example, some women grow up playing the role of "Daddy's love" while also being a surrogate partner for

41

Mom. The last story in this chapter is about such a woman.
Men rarely have surrogate partnerships with both parents.

Women more frequently experience direct sexual touch
(overt incest) by their fathers while simultaneously playing
the role of a surrogate spouse. When this occurs, there is
a deep injury to a woman's core sense of self. The consequence to her in adulthood is a sense of living on an
emotional roller coaster, riding to the top of romantic
fantasies then plunging into the despair of romantic disillusionment. Feelings and reality remain insulated behind
illusions of loving and being loved. Her search for love is
driven and desperate, and a sense of union with men is
never felt except in the throes of passion. Underneath
this longing for companionship is a seething rage and contempt for the very object of her search — men.

DADDY'S GIRL

Vickie, a 37-year-old professional, externally was attractive, fashionably dressed, poised and articulate. She
had an air of confidence found only among the most competitive. In fact, Vickie's concern upon entering therapy
was that she knew how to attract and be competitive with
men, but she did not know how to "keep" them.

> Men always seem to be adversaries. I'm careful never to let my
> guard down around them. I often take pride and joy in seducing them
> sexually, then abandoning them. There is a certain victory in knowing
> that I'm wanted. I've always entertained the belief I had a right to act
> toward men as they do toward women. Using men was a rite of
> passage for me in becoming successful. Lately, though, I hate myself
> for engaging in the same behavior I've always despised in men.

Vickie spent her first therapy session examining her
self-contempt. Appearing agitated, she shifted the conversation to her most recent relationship.

> It seems when I do become interested in somebody, I manage to
> chase them away. Greg was no exception. Our relationship started
> out passionately, as all of mine do. There was something about Greg,
> though, that made me want more. I became consumed with him.

When I wasn't with him, I couldn't stop thinking about him. I would think about how he smelled, looked, dressed, what he might be doing at the moment, anything to keep me intoxicated with him. I rarely let my guard down with someone, but when I did, there was no stopping me. It was all or nothing.

I called him constantly and wanted to be with him every minute. He began to feel suffocated and wanted me to back off. I couldn't. His attempts to get some space from me only made me want to be with him more. Soon his withdrawal from me ignited rage. I attacked him and accused him of not caring. Later when I calmed down and realized what I had done, I would apologize and try to make up by being sexual. That pacified the situation for a time, but eventually that didn't work either. Greg spent less and less time with me. And my attitude became more vicious to the point where I did everything I could to emasculate him. The very man I had fallen so in love with now was the object of my hate. Finally he had enough and told me to stay out of his life.

Vickie's scenario with Greg reflected a pattern of relating to men that she had been frozen in for some time. Unable to hide behind her romantic and sexual illusions any more, her broken heart and lost chances for love consumed her. Women like Vickie approach relationships with a high degree of romantic intrigue which distorts perceptions about the relationship and the man himself. Instead of falling in love with the man, these women fall in love with the romantic fantasy. A spiral of disillusionment, pain and emptiness follows. Brokenhearted, following each lost love, the woman's desperation for romance and sexual excitement increases. It generally takes greater and greater distortion in perception to fit some man, any man, into the next level of romantic illusion.

Vickie went on to describe the pain and emptiness that followed her thwarted attempts at relationships.

God, I feel so depressed. I feel suicidal when relationships don't work out. I was so afraid of what I might do to myself after Greg dumped me that I realized I needed to be in therapy. I don't know why I even bother falling in love. I sometimes think it would be easier to see men for sex only and keep love out of it. Yet there seems to be a deep emptiness in me that longs to be filled with love.

> It's so difficult to admit I have struggles being close to men. Perhaps even more difficult is admitting I desire that closeness. I have always hidden behind a mask of professional competency, anger and competitiveness with men. As unfulfilling as it was, it was at least some way I could relate to men.

Vickie's defenses were no longer working. She could not sustain the pain and hurt of the abused little girl inside her. As in the other examples, Vickie's desperate, illusory and anger-filled attempt at relationships was her unconscious drive to bring to awareness and resolve the abuse she suffered as a young girl. The extremes in Vickie's behavior regarding men are common among women who have been "Daddy's little girl" or "Daddy's love" and who have been overtly sexually abused by the same man. A closer look at Vickie's relationship to her father reveals what underlies her pain and anger.

When asked to describe her parents, Vickie was quick to start with complaints of her mother.

> My mother was always bitching about something. I couldn't stand her. I couldn't do anything right in her eyes, she was always on me about something. Even though I had an older brother and two younger sisters, I always had the feeling she took special pride in criticizing me more than them. She seemed jealous of me and I couldn't quite understand that. I always felt like I must have done something horrible. I was always left feeling like a bad little girl around her.
>
> I don't have much memory of specific childhood events. In fact, I don't have any memories much before the age of five. After that my memories are filled with the constant antagonism between my mother and me. Life was a chore at home knowing I had to face her on a daily basis. My only pleasant memories were of my father. He seemed to love and adore me so much. If it weren't for him, I never would have felt any love growing up. Even though he drank some and maybe was an alcoholic, at least he had a heart.
>
> I loved and adored my daddy as much as he did me. We had a special relationship. He took me special places and brought home gifts just for me. At night I was the one who got to sit next to him or on his lap. I was always so excited to be around him. When we were alone, he told me how much he loved "his little girl" and if it wasn't for me, he would have left my mother long ago. All the while growing up, I knew I could be a better companion to my dad than my mother was. After all, I could tell he preferred me.

> My father was a favorite target of my mother's criticism when he wasn't around. She attacked him intensely when I was present almost as if for my benefit. She complained about his drinking and bitched that he spoiled me too much. I would defend him and argue back that I wasn't spoiled. She acted overly suspicious whenever I spent any time alone with my father and asked an endless number of questions. I always felt like I'd done something bad, that I was dirty. Being loved by my daddy had a price. Somehow I always was left feeling ashamed for receiving the loving attention I got.

When it was suggested that Vickie's relationship with her father was a significant reason for her pain and struggles in relationships, she protested.

> I can't see that. He was the one who loved me. I get sick to my stomach and frightened thinking about looking at my father's relationship to me.

After months of therapy, Vickie began to let herself in on the pain and violation her father's relationship to her had created. She also began to recover her memories from before the age of five. As weeks passed, Vickie had an intuitive sense that she had been directly sexually violated by her father. She began to experience a consistent dream in which "some dark-figured man keeps coming toward my bed, but I can't see his face; the dream always stops there."

One day Vickie came into her therapy session sobbing.

> I know who that man is. It's my father. I saw him in the dream last night. He sexually abused me. I can't believe it. It must have happened about age four or five.

Vickie's sense that she had been sexually violated became validated through her dreams. This occurs often with persons who have been sexually abused and have repressed the memory of it. Dreams become the avenue along which it travels to consciousness. Vickie had no memory of her childhood before the age of five as a result of her repression of the sexual trauma. When amnesia of select or specific periods of childhood is not a consequence of organic brain injury, it can be a symptom of sexual trauma.

Vickie worked through her pain and rage. She attended a women's support group for incest victims and received consistent validation in therapy of her "intuitive sense" that she had been abused. Her anger at her father that had been buried for a lifetime was expressed by her intense anger and seduction of men. Vickie had kept it hidden behind her illusion that her daddy was "all good and loving." Children who are abused have no choice but to create a false illusory image of the abusing parent. This enables them to believe they are loved. Children need to believe they are loved at any cost, much as they need food or water. For this reason children who are severely abused are always willing to forgive and love the abusing parent.

After the rage and pain subsided, Vickie was relieved at learning the reality of her abuse. However, breaking through the illusion created by her father's special attention of her was met with a struggle. She was willing to acknowledge she had been a victim of overt sexual abuse but not that her father's loving attention to her was a form of covert incest. After all, it was the only love she got, and it enabled her to remain on a pedestal above her mother, the parent she hated so.

Vickie's mother's suspicions regarding her time alone with her father suggest she either knew of or suspected the sexual abuse. Often the partner of an incest perpetrator knows of or suspects the violation. Vickie's mother likely kept her own feelings of contempt, shame and hatred buried behind fear and denial. Instead of confronting her abusive husband, she projected her hatred onto Vickie. Once Vickie began to recognize this, her feelings toward her mother changed. She began to think she wasn't hated by her mother after all. It was really her father that her mother hated.

Vickie also began to realize her father's seduction of her was a method he used to keep his wife's anger at bay. By keeping Vickie seduced in a "close" relationship, his wife was always left feeling jealous and competitive. The feelings of anger and pain about her husband's abuse became secondary to the importance of competing with her daughter. A competitive, covertly incestuous triangle was co-created by both parents. As Vickie began to see this, her childlike illusion of her father's love began to shatter. She saw him for who he really was.

Vickie's emotional roller coaster ride of romantic fantasy and intrigue followed by painful disillusionment was the consequence of this false image of her father. Her view of all men was filtered through this original distortion. Becoming attached only to the fantasy of the men in her life kept her father's seduction hidden. She never had to face the painful feelings required to live in reality rather than fantasy. Vickie now began to approach a relationship more realistically and see a man for who he was. The roller coaster ride was finally coming to an end.

The new stability in Vickie's life was assisted by her identification of herself as a sex and love addict. Through her attendance at support groups for this addiction, she realized she had created a pattern in her life that was out of control. In fact, as time went on, Vickie revealed more about her pursuit of sexual highs than she had first acknowledged. Her initial admission of driven romantic and sexual relationships was only part of the story. Vickie's history confirmed a pattern of sex and love addiction.

This description departs somewhat from the identification of sexual addiction which was discussed previously. Whether an addiction is defined as a sexual addiction or as a sex and love addiction is a matter of semantics. In some cases, though, describing one's pattern as both sex and love addiction is more accurate. This is more common among women than men. But many men who identify a sexual addiction are also driven in the pursuit of securing love at any cost.

THE PRINCESS

Although many women are overtly sexually abused, others who never experience that have been locked into a sexualized relationship with their fathers. Such was the case with Rebecca. She came into therapy complaining about her husband. This was her third marriage. None of her husbands had ever pleased her, and she had an endless list of complaints about each. Each of her first two husbands left the marriage because he "had enough of my complaints of dissatisfaction."

Although Rebecca made this statement, she went on to place the blame for the failed marriages on her husbands. She was unable to view her own behavior in context and see how she affected her husbands. Rebecca's blaming persevered as she proceeded to discuss her third marriage.

I seem to have picked yet another man who can't be intimate. Michael is just involved in himself. He never has enough time for me, and when he does, it's unfulfilling. I need something more. I sometimes think he doesn't even love me because he hardly pays any attention to me. I want to be loved and adored. Michael won't or can't do that. He claims he always makes it a point to set some time aside and connect with me when he gets home from work. But he only does it because I ask him to. I want him to do those things because he loves me. I shouldn't have to ask for what I want or need.

Besides, after he makes his perfunctory connection with me, he wants time to himself. He claims to be tired from working all day and wants to relax. I tell him that's my point, he never has enough time or energy for me. Sometimes I get so mad, I start screaming at him. I let him know if he doesn't start paying more attention to me, we're through. I want him to let me know I'm loved and special in his eyes. The lavish gifts he used to pour on me don't work anymore. I'm special, and I want to be treated that way. I guess I've come into therapy because I really don't want to have to go through another divorce, but Michael is just going to have to do some changing for it to work.

Maybe Michael and I need a long fun vacation together. Some place new and different. Perhaps I'm just bored. Maybe I don't really know what I want. I can't seem to feel satisfied about my life anymore. I'm starting to feel kind of empty. Maybe if I got pregnant, I would be happy. I bet a baby would adore me and love me. Then again, I couldn't do what I wanted when I wanted to. Having a baby might be too inconvenient. I know Michael wouldn't help out. Even if he did, he would have that much less time and energy for me. I'm confused. I want to feel special inside again.

Rebecca's delivery in describing her dissatisfaction was passionate and full of conviction. Though there was probably some truth that Rebecca chose men who had difficulties with intimacy, the truly relevant issue was her own intimacy struggles. As I continued to listen to Rebecca's complaints, it became apparent to me there was nothing her husband could have done to appease her. Her dissatisfaction wasn't really about him. It was about her own inner emptiness and longing for love that occurred well before she met Michael. Her desperation was evident when she switched back and forth between whether Michael or a baby or both could finally fulfill her.

However, Rebecca could not see this. She was convinced Michael needed to do something different so she could feel happy again. The inability to see her behavior in a more realistic context and to separate her own issues from those of the relationship was a consequence of an early childhood trauma. The trauma was that of never having been seen as a separate human being with different needs, wants, preferences, and feelings from one or both of her parents. The consequence of this in adulthood was a narcissistic reality. Rebecca could only see the reflection of herself in Michael. The fact that she became indignant that Michael wanted some time to himself after a long day's work reflects this narcissism. Her insistence that he was taking time away from her reflected the struggle she had in seeing that Michael could have needs or wants separate from her own.

Also the fact that Rebecca imagined having a baby might answer her need to be loved reflects her narcissism. It appears Rebecca would be unable to see her baby as having independent needs. Rebecca's injury is great. Her defense is to externalize, believing a vacation, a baby or an adoring husband would take away the pain of never having been loved and seen for who she really was.

It took many months of therapy before Rebecca stopped focusing externally on her husband as the cause of her unhappiness. She slowly began to realize her inner emptiness came from being seduced and abandoned as a little girl.

Rebecca had been her family's princess. On the outside she seemed to have it all. She was indulged by her parents and seldom held accountable for any misbehavior. Rebecca frequently received special privileges and rarely wanted for anything. Her siblings hated her, and her friends were envious. It was difficult to imagine that a child treated as so special could have been so deeply injured. She was adored by her father. As she described the specialness her father felt toward her, the emotional damage she endured became clearer. Rebecca's father treated her more like his mistress than his daughter.

As Rebecca began to recount her father's relationship to her, the "ickiness" of his seduction came evident to her. Though she had never been sexually touched in an overt way by him, Rebecca squirmed in her seat as if to get her father off her. She grimaced and exclaimed,

> My dad actually bought me sexy underwear. I can't believe it! I forgot all about that. It felt a little funny at the time, but he always said I was his "princess" and deserved the best. So I didn't think much more of it. Besides part of me liked being treated so special. When I started developing breasts, my dad would look at me with a big smile and proclaim, "You are becoming a woman." At that point he started taking me out shopping and buying me whatever I wanted. I'd come out of the dressing room with my new clothes on to get his approval. That felt funny, too, but I didn't think much about it since I really loved being treated so special.
>
> I've always been my dad's favorite. He paid lots of attention to me at home and wanted to know all about my day. I was adored by him and I knew it. I began to expect that from everyone in my life, especially men. He even talked about boys to me, telling me I should find a man who would love me like he did.
>
> Even as an adult, he continues to adore me. I almost seem more special to him than my mother. Last week when I was at their house, my dad wanted to go into the family pool for a swim, just the two of us. It felt kind of icky, but he said he just wanted some time alone with "his doll." That night when I got back home, I binged on food. The next morning I starved myself and exercised until I pulled a muscle. Throughout my life, overeating has been an off-and-on pattern. Sometimes I used to vomit or take laxatives as a way not to become overweight. I've stopped that, but now I'm into compulsive exercising and dieting.

Rebecca's eating disorder was another consequence of the sexually charged relationship her father had with her. Although she suppressed the memory of her father's seduction, her body continued to carry the feelings and sensations of this trauma. Her eating disorder masked her body's attempt to bring to consciousness the awareness of the sexual injury. The preoccupation with food and weight helped keep the reality hidden. Compulsive overeating, binging and purging oneself (vomiting, exercising or laxatives) or starving oneself are eating disorder patterns common to victims of covert as well as overt incest. The energy spent focused on food and weight leaves no room for the body to heal. As Rebecca began to validate her inner reality of being a covert incest victim, the compulsion to overeat slowly subsided. She also needed the support of Overeaters Anonymous to help her overcome her compulsion.

It was crucial that Rebecca directly address both the compulsive eating pattern and the root cause of the compulsion. There is an unwritten rule expressed from time to time by members of Anonymous programs: Understanding the reason behind the addiction is not important. One is sometimes encouraged to use the support and philosophy of the Anonymous program and forget the "why." Though there is some merit to this belief in the early part of recovery (stopping the compulsive behavior and making one's life more manageable), it actually is a hindrance to ongoing recovery (peace of mind, comfortableness with one's own body and self, and emotionally fulfilled and functional relationships with others). It has been my experience that those people who give in regularly to their addiction (be it food, sex or gambling) are the ones who remain in denial about the root injury that opened the way to the addiction in the first place.

The preoccupied relationship Rebecca's father bestowed upon her was motivated out of his needs, not hers. Rebecca was seduced into a sexualized, idealized relationship with her father, believing his special attention was all she needed. Simultaneously, she felt emotionally abandoned.

Her legitimate needs for love, belonging and separateness were never met. Being adored and admired were her only clues to the mystery of what it would finally take to fill up the restless, empty space that lay in her soul.

Rebecca's narcissistic reality was her prison. By continuing to complain that Michael wasn't paying enough attention to her, Rebecca hoped to recapture the specialness she once felt as Daddy's princess. Yet it was this very focus that kept her from realizing the true emotional injury which resulted from being treated in such a special way. No one was ever going to be good enough for Rebecca. She was still in love with her daddy. As Rebecca faced the reality of her father's relationship to her, her emotional freedom began. Her experience of grieving the emotional losses she endured as a little girl finally allowed her to accept the fact of her father's seduction. The true reality of her childhood was the key for which she had been searching. Her heart finally started to heal.

The narcissistic reality present in Rebecca's story is a common, almost universal consequence of being a covert incest victim. This is of course true for both men and women. Since the covert incest victim is never really seen by the parent as uniquely separate, she in turn has difficulty acknowledging the fact that significant others in her life have needs of their own. Essentially, to varying degrees, covert incest victims see the world revolving around them. Correcting the distorted perceptions inherent in such a reality is a major issue for all covert incest victims.

It bears mentioning that Rebecca's father was probably sexually obsessed and most likely addicted. He violated significant boundaries with his daughter. This suggests his own inner reality was lost to sexual intoxication. It isn't parents' feelings of attraction toward their children but what they do with those feelings that becomes potentially violating. Many parents have feelings of attraction toward their children. That in itself is not damaging. It is in the sexualizing of the child that the violation occurs.

Rebecca's parents had chronic difficulty in their marriage. Both participated in making Rebecca the princess.

Her mother indulged her as well, though it is apparent Rebecca received more "loving" attention than she did. But by participating in keeping Rebecca her father's princess, she did not have to deal directly with the problems in her marriage. Both of Rebecca's parents used the sexualized relationship between father and daughter to avoid dealing with the dissatisfying expression of intimacy and sexuality in their marriage.

FATHER'S LOVE AND MOTHER'S SURROGATE HUSBAND

Playing the role of a surrogate spouse to both parents is devastating, perhaps the most tormenting of the situations presented so far. The result is a loss of clear identity. One's inner life feels empty and agonized. Awareness of feelings, choices, preferences, wants and desires is lost under a deep sense of unworthiness and inadequacy. Outwardly, these women seem to be able to do it all. They also are capable emotional caretakers of others. They leave the impression that they have few cares of their own, and if they do, they handle them just fine. Yet there is great pain in the experience of self for these women. They have contempt for their own femininity and fear men as well.

In an alcoholic or dysfunctional family, it is often the eldest daughter who occupies this dual role. However, it is not limited to the oldest. Any number of circumstances can change that. The middle daughter could be both parents' favorite and be seduced into a covertly incestuous relationship with them. Or it could be the youngest daughter who is trapped by the progressive dysfunction or alcoholism. Dysfunction in a family progresses. It never stays the same. As it progresses, appropriate boundaries between parent and child may become nonexistent and communication between parents increasingly strained. If an older daughter isn't already a surrogate spouse (or has left the home), the youngest has no choice but to pick up the slack. Often the departure of an older sibling leaves younger siblings vulnerable to covert incest. This does not mean that the incestuous bond between the oldest sibling and parent is severed, but that there are now more players in the drama.

Sue happened to be the oldest daughter in an alcoholic family. She came to see me because of ongoing difficulty in her current relationship. Sue immediately took command of the therapy session by offering a concise description of her family. It seemed so well thought out, I guessed Sue had more to hide than reveal. She described her family dysfunction in a way that suggested she had handled it well and put it all behind her.

> My dad was the alcoholic. He wasn't a bad drunk, but he did drink a lot. Sometimes he would get wild with rage, screaming and yelling at me or my mother. I was afraid of him at those times and stayed away. When his attacks were over, he was always sorrowful. He looked like such a little boy, I would try to comfort him. It was hard to stay mad at him.
>
> Though I was afraid of him at times, I knew I was special to him. His nickname for me was "Daddy's love." He would frequently let me stay up late with him after everyone, including my mother, had gone to bed. I would sit on his lap with my arms around him while he talked about his day. He talked of my mother frequently. He talked about how unhappy he was with her and that he wasn't sure why he married her. He used to tell me I must have been the reason he married my mother. He often added he thought I was the only reason he stayed married.
>
> After our talks at night, my dad would put me to bed. This was my favorite part of the evening. He would lie down next to me and hold me. Sometimes he told me stories or just how much he loved me. I loved it when he fell asleep with me. When I awoke in the morning, he was always gone. At times I felt like I had done something wrong because he didn't stay. I really felt ashamed. When he stopped putting me to bed, I felt I'd done something wrong. I'll never forget it. I was about 11 or 12 years old when he kissed me on the cheek one night and sent me off to bed without our special time together. From that point on, there was never to be any special attention from him at bedtime. No explanations were ever given. I thought for sure I must have done something wrong. Even to this day, I'm still not sure what happened.

Sue sounds more like someone confused by a lover's departure than a woman trying to piece together the fragments of a father-daughter relationship. His sleeping with her at night was highly sexual, although his intentions were likely only to show affection. It is probable that at 11 or 12 years of age Sue began to develop and mature as a woman. Her father might have feared his own feelings and become aware his behavior was inappropriate. Without an explanation, Sue was left feeling at fault for the abrupt change. This brought a deep sense of shame to her sexuality and growing womanhood.

Throughout her teen years and adulthood, Sue's father remained special to her. Though there was no more bedtime closeness, the two continued to have long talks together. Of her parents, Sue's father was the one she turned to for love and support. She knew he loved her. She was less certain about her mother, though they were close as well.

> At night I was very close to my dad. By day it was a different story. I was my mother's best friend, what seemed at times to be her surrogate partner. I provided emotional support and comfort when my mother was feeling depressed, which happened often. If I thought she was sad, I made her breakfast in the morning after my dad left for work. I would tell her not to worry, that I loved her very much and everything would be all right. She talked a lot about her problems, primarily about my dad. Even though I felt that my dad and I had a special relationship, it was hard not to side with my mother also. She seemed so lonely and unhappy. It was hard not to want to comfort and console her, though I hated to at times. I resented the fact that I was her sounding board.
>
> My mother didn't show me the kind of love my dad did. But she always needed me and I figure she must have loved me. Sometimes at night we went out together to a movie or dinner and left my dad at home. She said he didn't want to do those kinds of things. I felt torn between them. It was hard to know who to side with. I felt important to both of them. I felt particularly uneasy when my mother complained about sex. She said my dad didn't want to have sex with her or couldn't have sex with her. I don't remember what the exact words were. I do remember when they fought, it was often about sex. I think my dad had some sort of sexual problem. I felt terribly guilty, like I was somehow at fault.

Sue appears to have felt like the "other woman" as a little girl, interfering with her parents' sex life. This only added to her sense of shame regarding her own sexuality. Though the relationship was more obviously sexually charged with her father, the relationship between Sue and her mother had the makings of a sexual exchange. Sue was made to feel that she was replacing her father. The sexual energy was transmitted through the emotional caretaking between Sue and her mother. Having to console her mother when she complained about sexual matters likely left Sue feeling as if she had betrayed her father.

Relatively speaking, Sue idealized her father most and had more difficulty with her mother. However, this split in loyalties between parents was not as apparent as in the previous stories of covert incest. As dysfunctional as it is, having split loyalties provides some refuge for the covert incest victim. She has a channel for her feelings in seeing one parent as all "bad" and knowing she is loved by the parent she sees as all "good." She takes the side of one parent, thus allowing some sense of relief from the anger and rage. This was not an option for Sue. Having been a surrogate partner to both parents, she felt at war within herself. Her inner core — her sexuality — was the battlefield.

This inner battle is apparent in Sue's description of her relationships with men.

> It seems like in one relationship after another, there is some problem with sex between us. I feel like the men I draw into my life are either preoccupied with sex or somehow feel uncomfortable with themselves sexually. The last man I was involved with had difficulty being sexual. Although John was initially charming, he didn't express a lot of passion. In fact, he seemed void of it, and I didn't feel a lot of passion toward him. I felt more sorry for him. It was almost as if my attraction toward him was based on pity. Even the times we were sexual, it was more obligatory than exciting. Finally the relationship sort of just dissolved, without any major fighting. I felt relieved. I had begun to feel guilty and burdened, believing somehow I was at fault for his sexual difficulties.

The re-creation of Sue's relationship with her mother is apparent in the relationship with John. She confuses love with pity and has a sexual relationship based on guilt and

obligation. These are the rudiments of the surrogate partnership with her mother. Sue's attraction to men with
sexual difficulties is her attempt to re-enact the relationship with her mother and finally separate from her.
Though there was never any overt or apparent sexual
expression from her mother, Sue's pattern clearly ex-
presses that the relationship was sexually damaging at
some level.

Sue went on to describe her current relationship.

> Dave is totally the opposite of John. He is very passionate, too much
> really. He is the other extreme. It seems like this is a pattern; a dispas-
> sionate relationship followed by a highly passionate one. Dave seems
> obsessed with sex. I do things with him that I would never think of
> doing on my own initiative. Though I feel uncomfortable with some of
> our sexual behavior, I go along with it anyway because I know he
> loves me a lot. After all, he always wants me. Dave has a high sex
> drive. We make love every evening before we go to bed, no matter
> how I feel. This is our special time together. Even when we are done
> being sexual, he often masturbates himself. I feel like somehow I don't
> satisfy him. I am willing to do anything he wants to satisfy him. Recently
> we've been watching pornographic movies together. This brought me
> a lot of shame and was the catalyst in helping me seek therapy.

Sue's relationship to Dave is the re-creation of the seductive relationship with her father. This is the other side
of the battle she was caught in as a young girl. Regardless
of her father's intentions, his affectionate behavior toward
Sue was perceived by her as sexually charged. One of the
consequences for Sue in adulthood is to affectionalize
sex; that is, to regard exclusively sexual behavior by a
partner as a sign of love or affection. This trap invites
men who are sexually addicted into the lives of women
like Sue.

Sue is a co-sexual addict. A co-sexual addict is a person
who has a pattern of attracting sexually addicted partners
and violating his or her own value system to please the
partner. What drives this is the longing for love and the
belief that sex is exclusively a sign of love. One of the key
distinctions Patrick Carnes makes between the addict and
co-addict in his book, *Out of the Shadows: Understanding Sex-*

ual Addiction, is in the belief system. Addicts believe sex is
their most important need, and co-addicts believe that sex
is the most important sign of love.

Sue, who felt tremendous guilt and shame regarding
her sexuality, readily violated her own value system in
hope of satisfying Dave. She hoped finally to feel loved
and special again as she had with her father at bedtime.
Certainly the compulsion to be sexual nightly regardless
of how she felt was Sue's attempt to recapture what that
11-year-old little girl lost. But she never received what she
longed for. She wanted to be loved as that little girl de-
served to be loved, for who she was, not for the comfort
she provided her father. Pleasing Dave sexually was never
going to fill her void.

In addition to therapy, Sue joined a support group for
men and women involved with sexual addicts (see Appendix for a listing of these groups). In the beginning Sue
focused on Dave as the cause of her shame and the feelings of humiliation she experienced. This is a common
reaction of co-addicts. Because of the sense of violation,
co-addicts tend to regard the addicts in their lives as the
cause of the shame. Although being involved with a sex
addict leads to direct humiliation of some degree, co-addicts don't typically become that way because of the addict.
The co-addiction has its roots in childhood, not in adult
relationships. Co-addiction is a compulsive pattern where
there is an external focus on another (typically one's
spouse) as either the cause or cure of feelings of incom-
pleteness and unworthiness.

Sue projected onto the men with whom she became
involved her own unresolved childhood trauma and sexual
shame. It wasn't until Sue focused on what happened to
her as a child rather than as an adult that she finally began
to break the bond of addictive relationships.

Co-addicts who remain exclusively focused on blaming
others for their relationship struggles only re-create another similar situation. Only the names and faces will be
different. Sue's life clearly reflects that her relationships
were a choiceless pattern that could only be broken by

looking internally. Sue had to acknowledge her anger, rage, shame and guilt about both her parents. Over time, her own sexuality stopped being the battlefield for a war that should never have been hers.

Co-sexual addiction does not have its origin in only a background like Sue's. It can occur with any of the backgrounds presented so far. In general, it seems more women than men become co-sexual addicts and more men than women become sexual addicts. However, there are many women who are sexual addicts and men who are co-sexual addicts. What is clear thus far is covert incest affects one's sexuality. This is true for both men and women.

When Does Sex Become
A Hiding Place?

At the center of every addiction, as at the center of every
cyclone, is a vacuum, a still point of emptiness that generates
circles of frantic movement at its periphery.

Peter Trachtenburg
The Casanova Complex

To become addicted to sex is to become enslaved by one's very existence. Sexual addiction feeds on itself. Each compulsive sexual activity leaves a hunger for more. For the addict seduced by the illusion that sex will fill the emptiness, the most natural of all human desires becomes a source of desperation.

In its extreme, sexual addiction is life-threatening. Pursuit of new sexual highs becomes the primary purpose of life although the experience of feeling alive progressively erodes. One is imprisoned by one's own desires. Each attempt at sexual pleasure brings hope for freedom. As the search continues and the risks increase, hopelessness grows. Locked away, the spirit withers and dies. Such is the plight of the compulsive masturbator who risks auto-erotic asphyxiation, the womanizer who wakes up next to his best friend's wife only to consider suicide as an option, or the high school teacher whose string of one-night stands leaves her the victim of a deadly attack by a man she barely knows.

The addiction need not be at these extremes to cause deep suffering. Early on, the addict regards excessive sexual appetite as a way to self-definition. Soon sexual activity becomes a hiding place rather than a source of genuine love and intimacy. Sexual addiction insidiously depletes self-worth, integrity and hope. In the wake of its destruction lie despair, confusion, anger, guilt and shame. Addicts are emotionally unavailable to themselves and to those around them. Relationships with significant others are distant and strained. The one place addicts usually seek refuge — work — eventually begins to be disrupted as well.

Sexual addiction has many forms and does not discriminate based on gender, sexual orientation, race, class or occupation. It can be as natural and seemingly benign as masturbation or sex within a marriage. Or it can be as damaging and victimizing as incest or rape. Not all rape and incest are committed by an out-of-control sexual addict, yet some sexual addicts commit incest or rape. Conversely, not everyone who masturbates, has an affair, engages in one-night stands or uses sex to avoid conflict is a sexual addict. However, sexual addicts can and do engage in any or all of these behaviors. A sexual addict can become a prisoner to any of the following: masturbation, pornography, multiple relationships, anonymous sex, affairs, prostitution, transvestism, indecent calls and liberties, voyeurism and exhibitionism. A more thorough discussion of the different behaviors of the sexual addict is given in *Out of the Shadows: Understanding Sexual Addiction* by Patrick Carnes.

The public is more than willing to label the incest perpetrator, voyeur or exhibitionist as perverted and sick. The prostitution or pornography junkie is condemned as illwilled or amoral. But patterns of affairs, multiple relationships and sexual conquests rarely raise an eyebrow. In fact, they are normalized and romanticized.

Yet many of the normalized and romanticized sexual behaviors in our culture have the hallmarks of sexual addiction. These include:

- Secrecy
- Sexual obsession (e.g., a constant fantasy-filled stream of consciousness)
- Ritualistic behavior (e.g., a certain style of dress) used to enhance sexual excitement or conquest
- Sexual behavior used to avoid reality and feelings (or used to create feelings when there is an absence of feelings in day to day living)
- Tolerance, needing increased risks or stimuli to achieve the previous level of sexual excitement. However, in some cases tolerance may not occur and the addict may have a stable baseline of addictive behavior.

A more detailed discussion of this pattern of sexual addiction can be found in *Contrary to Love: Helping the Sexual Addict* by Patrick Carnes.

Tolerance does explain an escalating pattern of sexual addiction. Tolerance occurs in either fantasy or behavior. For example, an addict using benign fantasies to become sexually aroused may progress to needing sado-masochistic fantasies. Or the addict may switch from fantasies to behavior when the fantasies reach a level of tolerance. The adulterous spouse, whose sex with a partner across town no longer gives the kind of risk and excitement it once did, might bring it closer to home by becoming involved with a good friend's spouse. When the excitement of the risk wanes, the addict may become careless in keeping the affair a secret. Examples are endless, but all share the same common thread of tolerance. Tolerance is what drives addicts to violate values, convictions and promises. The end result is one of destruction and pain for both addicts and their loved ones.

In the case of a covert incest victim, sexual addiction is a misguided attempt at separation and definition of self. The sexually addictive behavior becomes a perceived gateway to feel separate from the opposite-sex parent and experience an autonomous sense of self. Not all victims of covert incest become sexual addicts, nor are all sexual addicts covert incest victims. Nonetheless sexual addicts often played the role of a parent's surrogate partner. The entrapment inherent in this covertly incestuous relationship leads to a pattern of addictive pursuits of sexual and romantic highs. These highs offer the covert incest victim an escape. This temporary escape creates an illusion of freedom which helps fuel the intensity of sexual pursuits.

Covert incest victims seldom experience life as spontaneous and guilt-free. Rather, they are burdened with a sense of never doing or being enough and are removed from the real or true inner life of who they are. Early on they realize their only source of self-worth rests in sacrificing their own needs and feelings to the emotionally vacant and seductive parent. For a child there is no choice in this — it is a matter of survival. Yet these children intuitively know and as adults are consciously aware of the murder of their souls.

Not surprisingly, a murderous rage toward the opposite-sex parent festers. Occasionally, when the rage grows beyond tolerable levels and the ego boundaries collapse under the strain, the murderous feeling finds direct expression.

After Ray is apprehended for a series of systematic violent rapes which left two victims dead, his neighbors are shocked. The newspaper article about Ray includes a comment by a disbelieving neighbor: "I've known Ray and his mother for a long time. I can't believe this. Ray has always been a good boy. He lives with his mother and takes good care of her. He is always by her side. They must have the wrong man."

True, this is an extreme example, but it does occur. The more systematic and ritualistic a rapist is, the more likely sexual addiction is a factor. This is not in defense of the rapist, but an attempt to make a point using the extreme case. Furthermore, the more seductive, entrapping and violating a mother's relationship to her son, the more likely that son will be to express aggression toward women, rape notwithstanding. Such was the case with Ray. He was indeed a good boy and close to his mother. Too good and too close. The more a man feels unable to separate from a covertly incestuous relationship with his mother, the more likely his sexual behavior will become addictive and victimizing.

The remainder of this chapter takes a look at the lives of three sexual addicts whose stories are less extreme than Ray's. However, they clearly highlight the role of a parent's seduction in developing the pattern of sexual addiction. Further, the stories demonstrate how covert incest contributes to the double or "split" secret life of sexual addicts. These men and women often hide behind a public life of success and high achievement. The following stories include a politician, minister and corporate businesswoman.

I chose three individuals who have a high profile either in the community or in their profession. My hope in doing so is to help explain why people who appear to have it "so together" on the outside actually have a secret sexual life. It is important to remember that one need not necessarily have sexual indiscretions reach the level of a "public scandal" to be a sexual addict. There are as many styles and types of sexual addicts as there are brands of alcohol different alcoholics prefer. As the underlying process is the same for all alcoholics, so is the process of sexual addiction.

WILL, AGE 47, POLITICIAN

Will was a man who, on the surface, had it all. His political career was taking shape. His hard work in state and local politics was paying off. His campaigning had led to national office and the likelihood of re-election. He had a successful, growing career, a warm and loving wife and three wonderful children.

To friends and family who knew his childhood, Will seemed a miracle. Although he came from a successful upper-middle-class family, his growing up years were filled with strife and neglect. Among the family, Will's father was known to "like his bottle and his women" and his mother was seen as bitter but forgiving. Will vowed early never to be like his father and quickly filled his father's shoes by being at his mother's side. Family members often commented on the way he was always the "politician" of the family and so strong since he weathered his parents' troubled marriage so well. Will's career, wife and children were proof he had survived the hidden inner struggles of his early family life. In fact, friends and family privately commented, "He has risen above it."

Then one morning when Will picked up the paper, the headlines and a front page photo were about him and his lover. Will was filled with rage and shame. He had been involved for months in an affair with a woman he met at a political function. Will thought he had kept it secret enough so he wouldn't get caught. After all, his wife, Mary, said she would divorce him if he had another affair. This was not Will's first affair and he had a reputation as a "womanizer" and "flirt." As he sat and stared at the paper, Will couldn't believe he had been photographed with his girlfriend in front of his apartment in Washington, D.C. He had forgotten he had taken her there, something he always avoided previously with her as well as the other girlfriends. Stunned, he didn't understand why he took that risk. "Maybe I wanted to get caught," he thought.

Will's disbelief and questioning quickly turned to rage and blame. Someone was trying to ruin his career. Besides he figured he wouldn't have to become involved in affairs if he and Mary were more compatible. Will frequently accused Mary of not being sexual enough. It was his reason for becoming involved with other women. The morning his latest affair was revealed was no different. After briefly expressing remorse and shame, Will launched into a tirade of blame and rage. Although Mary had heard it all before, she couldn't separate herself from her husband's accusations. As she always did, she believed his blaming and felt her own shame. Mary wanted to demand that he leave, but her shame paralyzed her and left her unable to act in her own best interests. Instead, she agreed to play the role of the dutiful wife at her husband's side the following day when he would have to explain himself to the press. This cycle of shame, blame and minimization is common to sexual addiction.

As the press fired questions, Will denied the affair and Mary claimed he was a faithful husband. As the days passed, however, more evidence surfaced, including an admission by Will's lover. Since the truth could no longer be denied, Will attempted to minimize its significance. But the damage was done. Will's political career was over.

Tolerance and progression help explain why Will risked bringing his lover to his apartment where he must have been aware he could be watched. It isn't so much that he wanted to "get caught" as he initially believed (addicts try to cover up and hide their behavior, not reveal it), but the insatiable appetite of the addiction drove him to seek riskier situations to increase the "high" of the experience. Sexual addicts are addicted to the mood alteration the high offers rather than the actual sexual behavior itself. The need to feed the addiction interferes with any conscious awareness of the consequences of the action. When consequences surface, the mechanism of denial serves to circumvent the awareness. It might not be farfetched, for example, to imagine Will thinking, "I won't get caught. I've got my tracks covered" and "What my wife doesn't know won't hurt her anyway."

For years Will kept his affairs, one-night stands and visits to old girlfriends, a secret. Mary knew of some of them and suspected others. Friends and co-workers knew Will strayed from time to time. Before marriage, he had a reputation for womanizing and was regarded as a Casanova. He regarded his major identity and purpose to be a womanizer. At some remote conscious level, marriage represented a chance for Will to end this boastful yet painful identity. Much to his surprise, marriage did not curtail his sexual pursuits. Instead it caused him to keep secret what he had at one time held out as a badge of pride and manhood.

Paradoxically Will's sense of manhood was inseparably tied to the experience of being romantically and sexually connected to women. He desperately needed the admiration, attention and company of women in order to feel adequate. Without it, he felt like a little boy. In fact, Will still was a little boy in the sense that he never emotionally separated from his mother. His romantic and sexual encounters offered him brief freedom from his mother's grasp and a chance to experience passage into manhood. Will described his childhood.

> I never received the support I needed from either parent. My mother's relationship to me kept me trapped. My father was never around. He was always drinking or chasing women. I felt I had no choice but to please my mother so she wouldn't leave me. The opportunity to be close to my father was never there. I was my mother's hero and golden boy. Even today, I still feel I'm trying to be her hero.

In the relationship with his mother, Will learned early on that his self-worth resulted from pleasing others, sacrificing his own needs and creating a public image of hero or savior. A life of politics was a natural place for Will to act out this role. It was a way to please his mother, feel good enough about himself and make the statement, "I am a much better man than my father."

Covert incest victims look to places and circumstances in life where they can mercilessly overachieve and attempt perfectionism. But they never feel adequate. They are ridden with guilt that they haven't done enough, shame that they "aren't enough" and rage that their needs are not met. The sexual arena offers a place to get a "quick fix" and be relieved of the burden of the covertly incestuous trap. As the striving for perfection grows, the hunger for adequacy and conquest in sexual encounters escalates. A double life is created and one begins to feed the other. As the shame of the sexual addiction increases, the striving to accomplish increases as well. This increases the very guilt, shame and rage that drives the addiction. It's a vicious cycle that feeds on the illusion of freedom and power the double life creates.

Will's political career was over. He had lost the respect of his wife, friends and family. Yet, his mother continued to defend her "wonderful son." Most importantly, Will lost respect for himself. He spent many days trying to bolster his damaged esteem by proclaiming, "I will make a comeback." He even gave a public apology in the hope of diminishing the public's mistrust. He vowed to himself and to his wife this would never happen again; he had learned his lesson.

The true extent of the damage from his behavior was not yet realized. Will's relationship with his wife and family was tense, shame-filled and combative.

> Life at home was miserable and I still blamed Mary. When I realized a political comeback would never happen, I became depressed. I felt inadequate and ashamed. For the first time in my life I thought seriously about suicide.

Since Will's political career was no longer a refuge from his inadequacy, he thought about returning to his sexual pursuits to get some relief.

> I couldn't believe I was considering getting involved in the very behavior that brought me down. I felt like an alcoholic who drinks to drown his sorrows from his drunken behavior the night before.

Will's story is typical of the life of a sexual addict. He struggled with being in therapy and wanted to try to do it by himself. Covert incest victims resist seeking help because they experience it as a sign of weakness. They often offer help, but seldom are able to receive it. The next story illustrates this more fully.

DAVID, AGE 41, MINISTER

David is a charismatic fundamentalist Christian minister who sought professional help as the result of an order
from his superiors. He had made a pass at the wife of a
church board member and was accused by another member of seeing prostitutes. His superiors were concerned
and did not want a public scandal. They gave David a
choice of either losing his ministry or seeking help. Reluctantly he agreed to counseling.

During the weeks David was relieved of his duties,
rumors persisted among the congregation. Accusations
increased. A number of women approached church board
members to tell their stories. All of them said the same
thing. David had attempted to kiss them or coax them
into having sex when they counseled with him regarding
personal problems.

One woman said she had an ongoing affair with David.
She tried to break it off many times, but he found ways
to coerce her to remain. With all the rumors circulating
about David, she was relieved to have a chance to clear
her conscience. The financial secretary also came forward
to report large amounts of missing funds that he suspected supported David's prostitution habit.

Other members of the congregation couldn't believe it.
They thought David was God's messenger and could never commit sexual indiscretions. After all, he preached frequently about sexual promiscuity and spearheaded groups
which fought against abortion and pornography.

"Sex," as David often preached, "is a sacrament between
a man and his wife and sin between everyone else. Unre-
pentant sinners will surely perish in the fires of hell." In
fact, David's most recent sermons were filled with dam-
nation for sexual sinners.

David's family life was also cited as evidence that the
accusations were false. His wife and daughters were never
allowed to discuss sexual matters or dress in a provocative
way. David was always on the alert for his daughters
showing signs of interest in boys or doing provocative

things, such as wearing earrings or lipstick. He would correct them and at times go so far as to accuse them of being "whores." David was making certain his daughters did not grow up to be loose women. Although David's wife went along with him, she too took the opportunity to confide to a church member that he was becoming obsessed with sex. He always talked at home about the sins of sex or raged at her with sexually abusive language. Lately he had begun accusing her of having affairs. She confessed she was beginning to feel battered.

Other church members said David was no different from other men and should be forgiven. "After all, God forgives him, so why shouldn't we? Just forget about it."

It isn't that simple. David is a sexual addict and to "just forgive and forget" helps perpetuate the addiction by not holding him accountable for his actions.

In initial therapy sessions, David was guarded and denied the reports from the church. After a time, however, he began to confide his story.

> I began masturbating at the age of seven to calm myself while my parents fought at night. My father was an alcoholic and often abused my mother. After he abused her, he had sex with her, sometimes forcefully. I couldn't understand this. I hated my father and vowed never to be like him. In the morning, after my father left for work, I would go into my mother's room and lie with her. I comforted her while she sobbed. She would say how sorry she was I had to hear the argument the night before and ask me to forgive her. Together, we discussed how terrible my father was. I felt powerful when my mother assured me I was her savior and her only support through the rough times with my father.

David's close relationship with his mother continued and his contempt and disgust for his father grew. David's own secret life with masturbation also progressed when he discovered his father's pornography collection.

> I began mutual fondling with boys and girls in the neighborhood. By the time I was an adolescent, I was obsessed with sex. I was also active in the church and often preached to my father about immoral behavior. Church was a place my mother and I went together without

my father. The anticipation for me almost felt like an adulterous romantic rendezvous.

Just before David was to go away to a Christian bible college to study to be a minister, he was accused of getting a high school classmate pregnant. He denied it, but she insisted. David's parents met with the girl's parents, who said she was going away to have an abortion and David was forbidden to ever see her again. David's father was enraged, but his mother protected him and claimed the girl must be lying.

Privately, David knew the girl had told the truth. Both he and his mother were relieved he would be going off soon to college. With a deep sense of shame and disgust for himself, he vowed he would never do that again and began faithfully to "serve the Lord." He was a model student and his instructors assured him the ministry was his calling. For a while David refrained from his sexually addictive behaviors with the exception of compulsive masturbation, which he decided didn't hurt anyone. Before long, because his masturbation fantasies no longer entertained him, he smuggled pornography onto campus.

David went on to describe his sexual life at college.

> The urge to approach women sexually on campus grew. I worried that if I got into trouble at school, I would ruin my chance for the ministry, so I started seeing prostitutes off campus. I reasoned this was okay because they were just whores and didn't interfere with my work at the school.

By the time he was 21, David was firmly entrenched in a double life. He had two worlds and was convinced they did not affect one another. When David's two worlds intersected, he panicked and briefly became conscious of his desperate sexual drive. In one of these moments he decided he needed to marry a good Christian woman to "put this all behind him." By the time he graduated from college, he was married. He promised himself and the Lord again that his secret sexual life was over. He had a wife, a clean start and was about to be appointed minister of a new church. David was certain things would be all right now.

Soon David was back into his pornography and shortly thereafter prostitution. Another promise and set of convictions had been lost to the addiction. When money ran out, he "borrowed" from church funds. Although they had two daughters, his relationship with his wife eroded. For years David kept both lives going. He began feeling tempted by the women he counseled. He was appalled and vowed to never act on this temptation. But as with so many promises before, his will was no match for the "sex-at-any-cost" drive of his addiction. Eventually he made a pass at the wrong woman, a church board member's wife, who did not hesitate to confront him and make his indiscretion public. At the age of 41, David's double life came to a screeching halt.

Although David did not see it at the time, this woman was a blessing. There comes a time in the life of all sexual addicts where they reach a point of "hitting bottom." That is coming face to face with the unmanageability and pain of the secret double sexual life. It is at that moment the addict is offered the chance to choose recovery and sanity. The only alternative is to go back into the denial and rationalization of the addiction and once again hit bottom. Because of the characteristic of tolerance, the next bottom will be more painful and unmanageable than the previous one. For some, however, there are no second chances. Sexual addiction can eventually kill.

David's story has all the characteristics of sexual addiction: secrecy, broken promises, denial and rationalization, tolerance and escalation, and violation of significant core values. David's addiction began, as many do, as a way to medicate feelings — the pain, shame and rage of witnessing his father's abuse of his mother. The covertly incestuous relationship with his mother began a life-long emotional bind which left no escape except for the illusion of freedom the addiction offered. The contempt and splitting off from his father and the joining sides with his mother began the development of David's capacity to live in two worlds.

One important aspect of David's recovery was to heal the split he had with his parents. This entailed David's searching his feelings to find compassion for his father, as well as finding the anger and hurt caused by his mother's seduction. David could more easily forgive his father than be angry at his mother. It was hard to be mad at a woman who took so much abuse. Yet he willingly acknowledged the rage and shame he felt for being his mother's confidant. He also felt tremendous abandonment from always sacrificing his needs to take care of her.

"It was no accident," David later commented, "that I became a minister." It was a role where he perpetuated the abandonment he felt early in his life. The caretaking of others left him feeling empty. The addiction was an attempt to fill up the emptiness. Abandonment is one of the most significant consequences of the covertly incestuous triangle and one of the main forces driving a sexual addiction.

Another important aspect of David's addiction is the deceptive nature of his public life. His preaching against sexual sins and activity in anti-abortion and pornography crusades was no accident since pornography and abortion were significant sources of shame and guilt in the history of David's addiction. Talking a *polar-opposite* position such as this is a common psychological defense against shame and anxiety. Freud first referred to this type of human defense mechanism as *reaction formation*.

It is easy to see how this contributes to the double life of a sex addict. Another example is the adulterous spouse who always harshly judges and holds in contempt those friends or acquaintances who have affairs. As the shame, guilt and anxiety of the secret sexual life increases, so does its opposite behavior. The more extreme, rigid and self-righteous one is in regard to an issue of morality, the more likely it is one has something to hide.

David and Ed are high profile individuals who received immediate public attention for scandalous behavior. It is not my intention to suggest all members of high profile public positions are sex addicts and covert incest victims.

Or that there aren't sex addicts and covert incest victims with ordinary jobs and occupations. Certainly there are.

However, it is important to recognize that helping and public professions (such as doctor, lawyer, therapist, teacher, clergy or politician) do draw covert incest victims into their ranks. After all, these individuals are invested in roles which fall into the helping and public professions; occupations in which giving, saving lives and souls, helping, and achieving are highly valued and rewarded.

The next story is about someone who does not hold a public position, but who is equally invested in the image of high achievement seen in the other two stories.

ANN, AGE 38, CORPORATE BUSINESSWOMAN

In the business world Ann was independent, self-assured and competent. It was rumored that she was soon to be one of the vice-presidents of her corporation. She was always careful never to mix business with pleasure, never dating anyone from work. Ann was viewed by coworkers as a strong woman. Even though they knew of her three marriages, they saw them as a sign of independence, of not necessarily needing a man. She was envied or held in contempt by the women she worked with, while the men sought her sexually or were intimidated by her. But no one suspected she had any secret life.

Ann entered therapy because her third marriage was failing. Her husband left her because she was having an affair with a business associate from a different city. This was the second affair her husband had discovered in the marriage. He had had enough.

Ann had never sought professional help before, but said:

> Maybe I have a problem. I can't seem to be satisfied with just one man. I thought by marrying Gary I would never have to be with another man. He seemed perfect for me and we had great sex. I can't understand why I did what I did. When I met Gary, I knew he was the one for me. The terrible loneliness that plagued me all my life . . . I was sure it would come to an end. Although I liked being with a lot of men, I was sure I'd be faithful to Gary.

As the weeks passed in therapy, Ann's story unfolded. And Ann did have another life. Though she had a clear rule of not dating the men at work, she actively sought out men who were in town briefly on business. She reasoned they had little or no direct impact on her day-to-day work at the office. She described a recent incident when a man from out of town doing business with the company approached her and suggested he had heard she "liked a good time." Ann was appalled. She realized even though she had one image at work, she was developing a different reputation elsewhere. She became paranoid and vowed never to see other men who were doing business with the company. "Besides," she confessed, "I'm not giving my marriage with Gary a chance."

Her resolution didn't last long. Ann met a man she couldn't resist. She reasoned it was safe because he had done business only once with the company and would not again. Ann also claimed this was different.

> He was somebody I really liked. It was more than just an affair. We really experienced intimacy together. I began to feel torn as to whether I should divorce Gary and be with him.

After a while Ann became careless. She permitted this man to call more frequently than she felt safe. Gary soon caught on and left. Ann felt ambivalent again. "Maybe I really want Gary now. I don't know what to think," she conceded.

Although she was independent at work, her history with men revealed her dependency. Her three husbands, she claimed, said her dependency was like that of a little girl. She hated to be apart and got extremely jealous when they wanted to be separate from her. Other times she accused them of having affairs. She demanded constant attention and love. Ann confessed, embarrassed,

> I wanted them to love me like my daddy loved me. None of them did. I feel like that's why I've been so disappointed in my marriages. And that's the reason I have affairs. If they loved me more, I wouldn't have had to see other men. But I always felt disappointed, so I sought other relationships to fill up the emptiness.

As a child Ann had been "Daddy's little girl" and she still was. She adored and admired her daddy and was adored and admired by him in return. Their relationship was special. Ann confessed she couldn't seem to love anyone like she loved her daddy. Ann grew up the oldest of four girls in a family torn by alcoholism and drug addiction. Her mother was an alcoholic and addicted to prescription drugs. In Ann's words:

> My mother was a Valium junkie who always seemed depressed and was overly dependent on me and my daddy. I had to take care of her and my sisters. I hated my mother. At other times I felt sorry for her. But not as sorry as I felt for my daddy. I knew he could never depend on her, so I always took special care of him. I filled in for my mother.
>
> I remember he took me on his business trips out of town. He was a chief executive for a big corporation and needed to go on business trips regularly. I stayed in the same hotel room with him and even slept in the same bed at times. But nothing ever happened. He never touched me except maybe to hold me sometimes. I got to go to some of his business meetings with him. I felt so special. I felt he loved me more than my mother. If it wasn't for my daddy, I never would have had any love.
>
> This went on until I was an adolescent and then it stopped abruptly. I felt so abandoned and lonely. I thought my daddy didn't love me anymore. I tried so hard to please him after that. I made sure I got good grades and always dressed up real nice for him when he went on his business trips. But I never got to go again. At the same time, my mother got worse and our family became more distant. I felt so alone and frightened. I started having boyfriends and being sexual with them by the time I was 13. That seemed to be my escape from the loneliness.

Ann began a desperate search to fill the vacuum created by the seduction and abandonment by her father, as well as the neglect from her mother. Here is where Ann's double life and the split in her personality between being overly independent and dependent had its beginning. She tried desperately to please and recapture the attention of her father. High achievement in school and dressing like a good little girl didn't work. Her feeling of abandonment grew and her desperation to find that special love to fill the emptiness escalated. Ann's secret romantic and sexual search began its painful course at the age of 13. Even then she had little control of the direction of her desperation. Any opportunity for innocence in the experience of her growing womanhood was robbed from her in the seductive, covertly incestuous relationship with her father.

Ann's story has themes similar to those discussed previously. For example, the nature of her secret life closely resembled the seductive relationship she experienced with her father. Ann became a corporate executive herself, engaging in affairs with men from out of town doing business. The most seductive aspect of the covert incest with her father occurred when he took her out of town on business with him. This is more than coincidence. Again it is the psyche's way of healing; recreating similar circumstances in adulthood in an effort to correct the experience and get the needs met that went unmet at those times. However, without conscious awareness of the abuse, the patterns repeat and repeat.

The pattern that developed in Ann's situation was one of sexual addiction, or more accurately, sex and love addiction. As mentioned previously, this difference is sometimes a matter of semantics. In Ann's case it warrants clarifying.

One way to distinguish between sex addiction and love addiction is to observe that the use of sex by sex addicts is an attempt to get high or alter mood. The sexual act is a fix for the sex addict, just as taking a drug is for the drug addict. In contrast, someone addicted to love may use sex in an addictive manner, but the purpose is to get love. Although there is certainly mood alteration in love addiction, the motivation behind the sexual pursuit is to attain love rather than get high. As already noted, both love and sex addictions can occur in the same person.

Certainly this was the case with Ann. At times she seemed indiscriminate in her sexual pursuit. At other times it became her gateway to intimacy. Additionally her extreme emotional dependency in her marriages and her romantic illusions reflected her love addiction. Her

romantic illusions have their roots in the seductive relationship with her father. Ann was always on the lookout
for someone to "love her like her daddy did." Ann
searched for the perfect partner to fill the extreme neediness and emptiness of the lonely little girl inside of her.
She consequently remained ambivalent regarding intimacy and commitment.

Ann's ambivalence is most apparent in her indecision on
whether she should stay in her marriage or her affair.
She believed she was creating intimacy in her affair, which
added to her confusion. Although there probably was
some degree of intimacy in her affair, it evolved within an
illegitimate context, shrouded with secrecy and shame.
This added to the bind of ambivalence for Ann. When
relationships have their roots in deceit, secrecy and shame,
addicts remain ambivalent and in conflict with themselves.
Such relationships have little possibility for healthy
growth due to the chronic ambivalence and shame inherent in their secret beginnings.

It is not uncommon to see people leave marriages or
relationships for affairs, only to find themselves faced
with similar circumstances. Only the names and faces are
different. In the recovery process from sexual addiction,
it is important for the addict to have honest and legitimate
beginnings in new relationships. It is crucial if an addict
has to leave a relationship that they become certain it is
the relationship they must separate from, rather than their
own inner conflict. Otherwise regret, shame and confusion prevail.

Another aspect which contributes to ambivalence regarding commitment is the unresolved grief from previous attachments carried into new relationships. This
unresolved grief becomes a source of conflict because it
inhibits new beginnings, never allowing a legitimate
chance for intimacy.

Ann has to resolve her grief and shame before she can
be clear about her commitment in her marriage. She will
also need to become willing to end her affair, which is

bringing her shame due to its illegitimacy. Ambivalence regarding commitment is a common struggle for covert incest victims.

The Struggle To Commit

But illusions are stronger than we might want them to be.

Henri J.M. Nouwen
Reaching Out

A child who has been a parent's surrogate partner suffers a deep emotional wound. The intuitive sense of self that permits the freedom and trust necessary to make constructive choices in relationships is damaged. In its place an idealistic illusion develops as to what relationships are and what they can provide. Hoping for a perfect partner or relationship becomes the criteria by which decisions are often made. Covert incest victims long to fill their illusions and feel their intimacy needs being met. Since perfection is not possible, never feeling satisfied becomes a chronic emotional response in relationships. Consequently the ability to make a full emotional commitment to a relationship is greatly restricted.

Typically the intimacy position covert incest victims maintain in relationships is one of ambivalence. "Sitting on the fence" or "having one foot in and one foot out of the door just in case" are common descriptions of this ambivalence. Wanting desperately to be loved and fearing it at the same time makes up the core of the ambivalence. The mask or outward manifestation of this fear is the search for the perfect partner. Until the core fear is resolved, the attachment to fantasy remains the only means to attempt intimacy. Tasting the sweetness as well as the bitterness of reality is never realized. Relationships become a string of disappointments which never live up to the expectations.

Ambivalence serves as a way to protect. By holding the ambivalence as a defense, covert incest victims stay guarded from the threat of being used and abused again. The original pain of being abused by the parent surfaces in relationships with spouses. As the need for further commitment in a relationship grows, the fear of being used again grows as well. Since the boundaries are often blurred between the incestuous wound of childhood and that of adulthood, being able to differentiate between one's spouse and the incestuous parent is difficult. Consequently the feelings of being violated become active. Ambivalence shields the covert incest victim from the threat of further abuse.

Although covert incest victims experience chronic ambivalence in relationships, the beginnings of the relationship are often quick and intense. Immediate and total commitment occurs, followed by the uncertainty of the ambivalence. The tremendous guilt the covert incest victims carry prohibits leaving if the relationship is not working. Instead they try to make it right, only to be disillusioned after each attempt. Or if the relationship has potential, the guilt interferes with clearly identifying personal needs to make a legitimate attempt to make the relationship work. Commitment becomes an arena desperately longed for. However, it is an experience which generates fear and confusion.

These hasty and intense commitments are born out of the attachment to fantasy as well as the tremendous neediness experienced by the covert incest victim. Rather than bonding with the person, the bond is to the fantasy the person represents. Since the fantasy represents the ideal or perfect person, the commitment is immediate. The person may have some of the qualities of the fantasy spouse, but in reality is never seen for who he or she really is. When the illusion dies, as they all do, the struggle regarding commitment surfaces. Now faced with who the person really is and realizing the vulnerability of committing so quickly, ambivalence sets in.

The other factor which contributes to the hasty commitment is the desperate hunger for attachment covert incest victims feel. Having been emotionally abandoned in the incestuous relationship leaves a tremendous neediness for love which consumes the search for a spouse. When this neediness is combined with the ongoing illusion or fantasy, the chances of making a relationship choice rooted in reality are minimal. When it becomes clear the relationship will not fill the longed for intimacy needs, the feeling of abandonment resurfaces. Additionally, covert incest victims blame themselves for the sense of failure and relentlessly search themselves for fault. They hope if they are scrupulous enough, they will find out what is wrong with them. Then they can change and make the relationship work. Guilt and confusion over their personal needs becomes pervasive. The pattern experienced with the covertly incestuous parent is repeated.

The guilt and confusion over personal needs lead covert incest victims to take cues from their spouses as to the needs in the relationship. Attempting to fill the spouse's needs in hopes of getting one's own needs met becomes a desperate pattern. Resentment, anger and hopelessness pervade. This pattern has its roots in the covertly incestuous relationship where the sacrifice of personal needs became the means of survival and hope for love. The identity development of the child — so crucial in developing clear commitments regarding sexuality, needs, values, wants, choices and feelings — is blocked. The adult capacity for healthy intimacy is lost.

JIM'S STRUGGLE WITH COMMITMENT

Jim's story reflects this ambivalent and painful struggle regarding commitment.

> I was the oldest of three boys in my family. My father was an alcoholic and a womanizer. He was seldom at home. When he was, he and my mother fought or were distant with each other. My mother was often depressed and demanding of me. I remember her trying to keep me close whenever she could. I felt guilty and responsible for her. I sort of took over the role of my dad in the house. When I did try to go out with my friends, my mother would often scream at me and hit me. I felt like I always had to take care of her needs.
>
> When I became an adolescent, she would comment on my looks or my body. It always felt seductive and icky. Even though I hated it, it also felt good to be so special in my mom's eyes. I found as I began to want to date that I was desperate to find a girlfriend so I could get away from my mother, but terrified at the same time.

Jim felt hurt and abandoned. He was terrified by his mother's rage. Consequently Jim was set up not to succeed in his relationships with women. A successful relationship would mean leaving his mother behind and potentially igniting her fury.

Jim's marriage was an attempt to correct and heal this early damage.

> I knew after our first date Cindy was the woman I wanted to marry. She seemed stable, clear, loving and trustworthy. She also had a strong commitment to family life. Cindy was perfect and I was going to make her my wife no matter what it took. My life had been a series of disappointing relationships and meaningless sexual encounters. When I met Cindy, I felt ashamed and unlovable. Knowing that someone like her loved me, seemed to take away my pain. After all of the ups and downs I had in relationships, meeting someone like Cindy was the answer to my prayers.
>
> Cindy's stability was important. I knew she would be consistent with her love no matter what I did. I never felt loved as a little boy. My mother's love always seemed conditional on what I could provide her. At best her care of and for me was inconsistent. Cindy was the

opposite of my mother. I knew she placed a high premium on love. If I married Cindy, my fear of being abandoned would be over. My dream of a perfect marriage and of a woman who would never hurt me was finally realized.

Though I knew we had some important differences, I fantasized that they wouldn't matter. Loving each other was what was important. In the beginning I worked hard at pleasing Cindy. I altered my thinking and feeling to some extent so we had fewer differences. I was willing to do anything not to lose her love. But soon reality set in. I began to feel resentful. I blamed Cindy and spewed anger and hate. The very person who was the object of my love became the object of my rage. Our differences became more important and began to matter. Love was not winning out. I felt confused and trapped.

I began to think about finding another woman. But I was married now, and I vowed I would never be unfaithful. I wasn't going to be like my father. But the pull became too strong.

I began a series of emotional affairs I would take to the edge by almost being sexual. When I realized what I was doing, I would stop, only to start a new emotional affair. Though I fought hard not to be sexual with these women, the energy I spent controlling it and pursuing them left me unavailable to my marriage. I became lost in the fantasies about these women and what they could provide that my wife couldn't. Masturbation became my primary sexual expression. Masturbation was the way I made my emotional affairs sexual. My anger toward my wife and the ambivalence about my marriage grew stronger.

Finally the pain became too great. I wanted to save my marriage and try again to live out my dream with Cindy. I entered therapy. I hoped if I could straighten myself out, I could love and feel loved as I always wanted. In that period I got my compulsive sexual behavior and fantasizing under control. I started feeling good about myself. But my uncertainty about the marriage grew stronger. I began sitting on the fence. Did I want my commitment? Or didn't I? I wasn't sure I wanted to live with her, nor was I certain I could or wanted to be without her. I was angry and confused.

The woman I thought perfect for me was someone I struggled to emotionally connect with. I began to feel the loneliness I felt as a child. Our differences, which originally didn't seem to matter, were clearly more important than I wanted to admit. My confusion and uncertainty increased.

Jim's rage toward Cindy was about his mother, not Cindy. When the fantasy bond with Cindy collapsed, his rage surfaced. Though he felt Cindy had let him down, it was his mother who had really done the damage. Being with other women was another way he expressed his anger and tried to stay safe. When the boundary between Jim's mother and Cindy became blurred, being with other women provided sanctuary from the potential of feeling abandoned again.

Jim's terror had also surfaced. The fact that he expressed himself sexually primarily by fantasy and masturbation indicates his need to stay in control and protected. Though Jim felt he needed to escape, he was careful not to give too much of himself away to these women.

Jim's ambivalence reflects the need not only to protect himself from the feelings of the covert incest wound, but also from the reality of the marriage. Jim and Cindy seemed to have important differences that made an emotional connection difficult. By choosing someone he was significantly different from, he could remain loyal to his mother and not have a successful marriage. This is an important and frequent dynamic that helps to explain the chronic dissatisfaction that covert incest victims experience in their relationships.

The tremendous guilt and confusion over personal needs covert incest victims experience prohibited Jim from making a clear choice to stay or leave the relationship. On one hand, Jim felt guilty when he considered leaving. On the other, he had too much confusion over his intimacy needs to make a legitimate attempt at bridging closeness with Cindy. Jim needed to work at identifying more clearly his intimacy needs before he could be clear.

Also the tremendous emotional dependency on Cindy left over from Jim's abandonment in childhood made it difficult for him to make a clear decision about the relationship. His story reflects the struggle between the needs of the inner child and those of the adult man. Ambivalence escalates when the needs of the inner child become the priority in an adult relationship. Covert incest victims often transfer the leftover needs and issues with their opposite-sex parent to their spouse. There is some validity to the notion that we marry our mothers or fathers. The next section looks more closely at how covert incest victims transfer childhood needs and issues to their marriages or significant relationships.

WHO DO WE REALLY MARRY?

As is clear so far, a covertly incestuous relationship results in many unmet emotional needs. Additionally, unresolved issues regarding guilt, autonomy and attachment are carried into adulthood. These wounds contribute directly to one's choice in a marriage partner. The notion that we marry our mothers or fathers is true when you look at marriages of covert incest victims who have not yet healed from their emotional wounds. They marry people emotionally like their opposite-sex parents in an attempt to work out these issues and heal the wounds. The hopes and illusions are so strong they prohibit the recognition that needs will again go unmet.

Invariably when I ask covert incest victims if their spouses are anything like their opposite-sex parents, the response is "yes." When they list the similar qualities, it tends to be the very ones these covert incest victims felt injured by with their parents. For example, it is common for me to hear comments such as:

> "My husband is emotionally absent just like my father was. I can't believe it; I thought I married someone different."
> "She's always making me feel guilty like my mother did. If I want to do something with my friends, I get the third degree. She hates me to have any separate needs from hers."
> "I feel like I have to take care of him like I did my dad. My husband's just like a little boy, and I'm his mommy. I hate it. I was my dad's parent."
> "She is always criticizing me like my mother did. I never feel like I'm good enough. I'm always trying to please my wife. It seemed I went right from trying to please my mother to trying to please my wife, who is never satisfied no matter what I do. I can't win!"

When this transfer of needs and issues from the parent-child relationship to the marriage relationship occurs, the capacity for healthy adult intimacy is limited. These relationships feel like parent-child or maybe brother-sister ones sexually and emotionally. The relationship may be passionless or extremely sexually and emotionally volatile. The incestuous bond is created all over again. The separation from the opposite-sex parent never really occurs; instead the same or similar attachment is transferred to the spouse. Covert incest victims remain little boys or girls in their marriages unless recovery occurs.

Rather than making an adult choice in a marriage, the inner emotionally wounded child of the covert incest victim does the choosing. It is easy to see how so many unrealistic expectations and illusions are carried into the marriage. The wounded child expects the spouse to be all the parent wasn't, often expecting perfection and unconditional love. However, the spouse is generally more like the parent than not.

Rather than choosing an emotionally mature adult, covert incest victims choose spouses who have been emotionally wounded in childhood. So instead of two emotionally mature adults striving to be intimate, you have two adults with childlike emotions struggling to be close. The quarreling and bickering is like that of two children on a playground fighting for turf. Sometimes these relationships are like two children, other times like parent-child in their interaction. The relationship rarely resembles two adults interacting. Satisfaction is seldom realized. After all, it is adults, not children, who create intimacy.

Still Trying To Please Mom

Dave and Marsha's story highlights the issues of transference of childhood needs and wounds to adult relationships. Initially Marsha came into therapy to complain about Dave not filling her needs.

> He always has his nose in the newspaper or is watching TV. He's so uptight I can't talk to him. I want him to take care of me and love me. But either he can't or won't. He is so insensitive to my needs. He's more open to the kids than to me. He's almost like one of the

kids. I feel like his parent more than his wife. Our sex life isn't that great either. I feel like I'm having sex with my brother. That's weird; I don't understand it. Sometimes I can't believe I married him. I wish he were different. I want to feel special and important to him. But I don't.

Marsha's complaints were endless. Her extreme focus on Dave left her little room to look at herself in the relationship. She was convinced Dave needed to do the changing and growing up. When I saw them together, their interaction was clearly that of a parent and a child. Marsha scolded and Dave got defensive or tried to placate. At those times Dave was a boy wanting to please his mommy. When he was able to muster any show of power as a man, it was done with rage. Then Marsha withdrew and became silent. In those moments she was a little girl pouting because she wasn't getting her way. Though Marsha complained of wanting Dave to be more of a man, at the same time she clearly was threatened by it.

Dave, on the other hand, seemed stuck in being a little boy. He described his oldest son as having more power than he did. In fact, the fighting between Marsha and her oldest son was more like two spouses than parent-child. They also had a daughter three years younger than their son. As they described their relationship with their children, it was clear that more of the passionate and emotional energy was directed toward the children rather than each other.

For example, it was common for the children to sleep with their parents, or for Marsha to fall asleep at night with her son in his bed and Dave to do the same with his daughter. Clearly there were problems in the emotional and sexual boundaries with the children, though overt incest did not seem to be present.

When Marsha was not in the session, Dave was more open and shared his feelings about the marriage. Even then he was guarded as if he wanted to protect Marsha and not complain too much.

Marsha's got a point. I'm certainly not very open with my feelings. I try to accommodate her and meet her needs. I tell you, if it wasn't for her telling me I wasn't intimate, I probably would never be able to be close. I really depend on her to guide me in the relationship. But there are times when I get mad at her. Although she may be right, she never lets up. She even criticizes me in front of my friends. And I just sit there and take it. I'm afraid if I get angry, she'll shut down and won't talk to me for days. She is so damn controlling. It's like she wants me to be open with my feelings, but on her terms — and that doesn't include being angry with her. I don't think I'll ever please her. Frankly I'm getting fed up with her complaining.

I have to admit, I feel like a little boy around Marsha. I hate it, but I don't know how else to be. It's almost like being around my mother, always trying to please her and be her helpful little boy. I'm afraid if I start being more of a man around Marsha, we won't have much of a relationship. Sometimes I just want to put her in her place and tell her to knock off the criticizing and complaining. But I'm afraid I'll lose her love. She's so much like my mother! Whenever I was even a little disobedient, my mother took away her love and approval.

As time went on, Dave talked more about his family. Clearly he was trapped in a covertly incestuous relationship with his mother. He was the youngest of three boys and his mother kept Dave at her side all his growing-up years. He was mother's good little boy and helper. As he described his incidents of disobedience as a child, it was apparent they were attempts at autonomy and not behavior reflective of a bad kid. However, his mother opposed any separate behavior and was critical of him as a way to control this separateness. This left Dave feeling guilty about his desire for independence. Having been abandoned by an alcoholic father, Dave relinquished his attempts at separateness to avoid being abandoned by his mother.

Dave grew up a good kid, never causing any trouble. He did whatever he had to in order to please his mother. Instead of going out with his friends after school, he went home and helped clean the house. He hated this but thought he should do it. Clearly Dave was controlled by a tremendous guilt and a deep sense of shame which left him feeling unworthy of his desire for separateness.

Then Dave met Marsha. Marsha was such a nice girl that his mother approved. Privately Dave knew marrying Marsha was his only way to get away from his mother so they married early in the relationship. But Dave never left his mother emotionally. Instead he essentially married his mother and recreated the same emotional relationship system with Marsha. There are many parallels between Marsha and Dave's mother, particularly the critical attitude and use of Dave to fill needs more appropriately filled by someone else.

In the case of Dave's mother, she used Dave to fill her need for her husband. In the relationship with Marsha, she not only wanted Dave for a husband but to fill her needs not met by her father. Her father was distant, cold and preoccupied — much as she described Dave. There actually were intimacy problems between Dave and Marsha, but her chronic complaining and never feeling satisfied were more likely about her father.

Dave and Marsha married their parents in each other. They also passed on to their children inappropriate sexual and emotionally passionate energy; energy meant for each other. Since emotionally they were both children, an intimate adult connection was a struggle. Connecting with their children became a primary means of experiencing intimacy. This is an example of how incestuous relationships are passed on from one generation to the next. Overt sexual incest between Dave and Marsha and their children remained a possibility. They both needed to emotionally separate from their parents to correct the boundary problem with their children and have a chance at intimacy with each other. The process of separation from parents and getting needs met will be discussed in the last chapter.

Does this mean that just because you married someone like one of your parents, you should get divorced? No. But it does mean you have to grow up emotionally to resolve the struggle with commitment and satisfaction in your marriage or relationship. It means both people have to be emotionally mature in order for intimacy to occur. If only one is, the relationship deepens in its parent-child feeling and becomes further removed from the chance of a satisfactory partnership.

Marriage should be a celebration of intimacy, rather than an attempt to fill the illusions of the abandoned inner child. I feel it is important for covert incest victims to stick it out in relationships long enough to make sure they are divorcing the right person. Too often I have seen the covert incest victim jump from one marriage or relationship to another. This is an effort to get separate from the leftover emotional bind with the parent, rather than clearly deciding the current relationship is not working.

WHO DO WE REALLY DIVORCE?

Another common relationship pattern for covert incest victims is to leave relationships too early. When things don't work out as they expect or when people begin to feel too close, they leave the relationship. They quickly begin to feel dissatisfied due to the illusions about love and romance. They don't stick around long enough to work things out and establish a mature relationship. Instead they divorce one partner and marry the next, expecting things to be different each time. However, changing partners does not change the inner reality of the covert incest victim.

This pattern is the struggle to remain committed. Here the covert incest victim never stays long enough to move from the attachment to the fantasy or perfect person to the reality of the individual. Instead of trying to bridge genuine intimacy, he or she bolts from the relationship, looking to bond with a new person but the same old illusion.

Covert incest victims need to stay long enough in relationships to allow the illusion to die and permit legitimate intimacy to develop. Until this occurs, chronic unhappiness and discontent remain. Covert incest victims often find themselves wondering if the relationships they abandoned would have worked if they had just "stuck it out." This adds to the ambivalence and makes it more difficult to commit to a new relationship.

The underlying issues of separation and attachment are never worked out when a covert incest victim gets divorced and jumps from relationship to relationship. Though poor choice in partners can be the underlying reason for multiple relationships, it can be equally true that the person who leaves is running from an inner struggle based on the fact that separation from the opposite-sex parent has never occurred. Thus, when he or she becomes involved with someone, all the pain, fear and rage meant for the parent surfaces. Rather than dealing with it, it is projected onto the spouse. The spouse then becomes the object from which separation must occur. In reality it is the parent the covert incest victim is attempting to divorce over and over again, not the spouse. Rachel's story illustrates this.

Is Divorce Inevitable?

Rachel was in her third marriage and in the process of divorce. She came into therapy because she was having second thoughts about going through with the divorce.

> I don't know if I really should do this or not. After all, this is my third marriage in less than ten years. I feel like I'll divorce Alan and find someone else and divorce him. I'm beginning to think something is wrong with me. I sometimes think if I hadn't had so many unrealistic expectations, my first marriage could have worked. I don't think I really ever got over my relationship with George. In fact, I was still involved with George when I started with my second husband. But I had some space between my second husband and Alan. If there's some way, I'd like to try to work things out with Alan.
>
> I don't want to be divorced again, but I've got some real problems with Alan. He's too demanding and seems clingy to me. Lately when he wants to be close, I just shut down. I don't want anything to do with him. At other times, I'm furious with him. He can't do anything right. I want something more out of this marriage and some kind of emotional satisfaction that I'm not getting.
>
> Yet when we do get close, I'm terrified. I don't want to be smothered like my dad smothered me. It was the same with each husband. I get too afraid to get any closer, but then complain that we're not close enough. Each time I manage to find a way to attack and blame the relationship. Soon we're fighting all the time and I'm complaining all the time. I can't wait to get out. Divorce always seems to be inevitable. I keep hoping my knight in shining armor out there will rescue me. I thought Alan was my knight but now I can't wait to get

away from him. I can't seem to stay committed and satisfied. I don't know what to think.

When I asked Rachel to say more about what she meant by not wanting to feel smothered like she was with her dad, she told her story.

> My father always had me by his side when I was growing up. I was his little sweetie. He and my mother didn't have much of a relationship so I was the object he adored. When I was younger, I enjoyed all the attention and closeness. But when I got to adolescence, I couldn't stand it. He never liked any of the men I dated, and he always asked me what seemed an endless number of questions about what I had done on my dates. Even to this day, he's always prying into my personal business about my life.
>
> He never approved of any of the men I married. It's like he never let me go. I really can't stand it. It feels icky to me, like I can't get away. I feel smothered by him. I just want to scream and run away. It's exactly the same feeling I had with each of my husbands at some point in the relationship. I start to feel smothered and want to run. And I usually do. I guess that's why I keep getting divorced. Sometimes I think all of my complaining is a way to justify my wanting to run from the relationship.

Rachel's story reflects the commitment struggle which leaves covert incest victims regretting past relationships. The regret generally is that the relationship might have "worked out" if a longer commitment were established. As Rachel's story reflects, the running from the commitment occurs when the relationship gets too close. It's at those times the injury from the incestuous relationship with the opposite-sex parent and abandonment by the other parent surfaces. At those moments, the pain is so great and the fear so overwhelming that running becomes an alternative. Without the framework of understanding, the damage of the incestuous relationship — feeling trapped — is experienced as originating from the spouse. The fear of losing what little autonomy and comfort the incest victim established pushes him or her out through the door. Multiple divorces or relationships are the pattern masking this struggle.

Once the withdrawal from the relationship begins, the covert incest victim uses the old illusion of finding the perfect partner to mask the pain and justify the withdrawal. In Rachel's situation, it was her knight in shining armor for whom she was looking. Her divorcing Alan was the beginning of another confusing, regrettable ending. Divorce was not the best alternative given the present circumstances. Instead it was necessary to stay with the pain and abandonment created by the incestuous relationship and separate from her father. It was also necessary to let go of the false illusions and expectations. Only then could acceptance and reality become the building blocks needed for intimacy. Letting go of the illusion has a grieving process of its own that adds pain to the pain of the incestuous injury. This is a difficult period for covert incest victims but necessary.

Afterwards Rachel was able to work through her struggle enough to commit to Alan and feel satisfied and comfortable, an experience she had longed for all of her life. As part of her process of recovery, Rachel had to say a clear goodbye to George, her first husband. Essentially she had been involved in an affair with her second husband and never finished her relationship business with George. This added to her confusion and inability to commit with Alan. Being involved in affairs adds another false set of realities and expectations to the struggles the covert incest victim has with commitment and desire for intimacy.

THE FALSE PROMISE OF THE AFFAIR

Becky was dissatisfied in her marriage for most of its duration. She never knew what was normal in relationships and assumed her dissatisfaction was the way relationships were. She and her husband were high school sweethearts who married right out of high school. He always treated her like a princess and was the sort of guy she always dreamed she should marry. Becky's father always treated her like his princess, so marrying Dan seemed right. During her therapy sessions, Becky acknowledged that marrying Dan was the only way she could get out of the house and away from her father.

Becky loved her father's attention when she was young. But as she grew into adolescence she began to resent it. In fact his attention became entrapping. She always felt guilty when she wanted to do things with her friends or when she started liking boys. She always felt as if she had to be at her father's side. Her father frequently made comments that left Becky with more shame and guilt. She recalled when she met boys, her father often commented, "Nobody's good enough for my princess." When she met Dan, Becky feared her father would not approve. But he didn't disapprove, so Becky stayed with Dan.

Becky described the marriage.

> Throughout our courtship and most of the marriage, Dan treated me like a princess the way my father did. He gave me everything I wanted and things he thought I should want. He was there for me at all times and made few demands. The only demand I sensed was an implicit one: "If I treat you this well, you are mine, I own you." Though he never said this to me, I always felt the expectation. It was the same expectation I felt with my father. I felt controlled. As time went on, I began to resent my husband's excessive attention to me as I did my father's.

Becky entered recovery for adult children when she sensed she had grown up in a dysfunctional family. She soon realized her feeling dissatisfied in the marriage was not normal. Becky also began facing the fact that her marriage was dysfunctional in similar ways to her family. Becky met Frank at one of the adult child meetings and they soon formed a close friendship. They had long talks over coffee after the meeting and talked to each other over the phone between meetings.

Becky discussed her relationship with Frank.

> I couldn't believe how I was beginning to feel for Frank. He was everything my husband wasn't. I was able to be myself. Frank never put any pressure on me. I was able to communicate and be intimate in ways I never had before. I fell in love with Frank. I eventually divorced Dan and continued my involvement with Frank. However, as time passed, our once free flowing and intimate relationship became

a battle. Frank stopped being the open and supportive person he had been. He became scared and ambivalent. In response I became desperate and clingy. We often fought without any sense of resolve. I couldn't understand how something so open and loving could turn out to be such a struggle. I felt trapped again, this time by my own desperation and fear of abandonment.

Having an affair is a way to be relieved of the struggle with commitment felt by covert incest victims. The affair becomes a place where they can be open and intimate in ways they have never been before. It is a means to escape the confusion and pain of the primary relationship without having to bring clear resolution. By moving out of the primary relationship into an affair, the original abandonment and separation issues are not engaged. Since commitment is not part of an affair, one's relationship issues do not surface. That struggle remains in the primary relationship, which is why affairs seem so carefree, open and intimate.

Since one's family-of-origin issues are not engaged, the affair becomes a relationship covert incest victims long for. It's free of the burden of responsibility of resolving the commitment struggle. But as reflected in Becky's story, the struggle with intimacy surfaced once the commitment in her marriage was severed by divorce. Her desperation for intimacy and feelings of abandonment created in the covert incestuous relationship with her father carried over from the marriage to the affair without adequate resolution. In a different way, Becky felt trapped again. The affair seduced her into believing there was a possible state of burden-free intimacy with Frank. It falsely promised her she would not have to deal with the drudgery of relating she experienced with her husband.

Does this mean Becky should not have divorced Dan? Not necessarily. Does it mean it would have been in her best interest to resolve her issues with her father and husband first before moving on to another relationship? Absolutely. Doing so provides clear resolutions and healing of the abandonment necessary to begin and maintain healthy and functional relationships. It frees one from having to deal with the possibility of regret for leaving someone with whom you might have been able to work it out. The possibility that Becky could find herself in the same bind with Frank as she was with her husband, and constantly second-guess herself about divorcing Dan, was a heavy burden to carry. It prevented her moving on in life and contributed to the ongoing state of ambivalence the covert incest victim experiences with commitment.

The last chapter details the steps necessary to separate from the incestuous relationship and begin building a more well-defined and whole self.

7

Toward Wholeness

*When you get married, 30 percent of your sexual energy may
still be with her [mother] and you got 40 percent for the woman
you're with . . . she's got about 40 percent with her father and
maybe 20 percent left for you . . . that's not enough.*

Robert Bly
Workshop, Power and Purpose in
Men, 1988, Oakland Community
College, Farmington Hills, MI

The primary task for covert incest survivors is
to separate from the opposite-sex parent. This
is not an easy step and may take years. The fact
that so many covert incest survivors remain inappropriately bonded well into their adulthood suggests a tremendous struggle to let go. This separation will not be
given. Real emancipation cannot be given. It must be

taken. Emotional maturity cannot be realized until emancipation occurs. You cannot be an adult man or woman
and simultaneously hold onto Mommy or Daddy. For a
marriage or relationship to work, full access to your emotional and sexual energy is necessary. Even then it's tough.
But, as Robert Bly's quote suggests, a relationship cannot
fully be functional when leftover sexual energy is tied to
the opposite-sex parent.

The other integral part of the separation is to heal the
relationship with the same-sex parent and allow yourself
to feel bonded. In fact, this needs to happen to separate
from the other parent. You need the identification and
bonding with the same-sex parent to stand separate from
the opposite-sex parent. This identification is necessary
to feel more powerful as a man or a woman.

However, most covert incest survivors have it confused.
They are still trying to feel good about themselves as a
man or woman by identifying with the energy of the
opposite sex. This cannot work. If a man is going to be
able to love a woman fully, he needs first to love himself
as a man. This begins with the father's love and continues
with the support and nurturance of other men. The re-
verse pattern is the case with a woman who bonds with
mother and other females to nurture the identity. However, covert incest survivors stay stuck in trying to please
the opposite-sex parent and spouse or partner as a way to
feel like a man or woman.

One of the patterns common to covert incest survivors
is the seduction and abandonment of the opposite sex.
This pattern leaves in its destructive path broken relationships, confused and hurt partners and lost chances
for love. Generally this is done unconsciously. It is a way
to get back at the seductive parent and gain a sense of felt
separateness, control and power. However, the attempt to
break from the seductive parent by seducing and abandoning members of the opposite sex can't work. The separation has to be directly from the parent. Following are
some suggestions to help foster the process of separation

from the opposite-sex parent and healing with the same-sex parent.

1. Let go of addictions. Addictions rob you of your sense of power and personal authority. They block you from your feelings and inner reality which are crucial to the process of recovery. Get help for your addictions in a specific 12-Step Anonymous program. Whether you're addicted to sex, food, alcohol or drugs, begin by making a commitment to attend a meeting specifically for your major addiction. You will need as much access to your sense of power as you can get in order to make the separation.

2. Let go of your idealized image of the seductive parent. Your parent's excess attention to you was largely for his or her own gratification. Acknowledge that the attention you received was violating and abandoning. You will also need to grieve the loss of this idealized relationship. Expect feelings of sadness.

3. Acknowledge your anger toward the seductive parent. Practice types of therapeutic body work such as bio-energetics. This is a constructive way to deal with the anger. Or write a letter to your parent, telling about your anger and your feelings of violation. It is usually best not to send the letter since this can be harmful — and this is not the goal of your anger. It is also important for you to write the letter without any sense of restriction. You want to feel free to let out as much anger as possible. Knowing your parent will receive it might inhibit you. Writing a letter is a productive way to deal with your anger if your parent is deceased. Go to the gravesite to read it aloud. This can be very healing.

4. If your seductive parent is alive, begin to set boundaries and separate. This is a crucial step. For example, if your parent continues to tell you about personal problems with the other parent say you are no longer willing to listen. Be prepared to set these boundaries more than once. Long-term boundary problems require a consistent and clear position on your part. If you feel icky, enraged or burdened by your seductive parent's request or conversation, those are feeling-cues that you're being drawn into the incestu-

ous role. Respect those feelings and set boundaries. If you feel guilty, which is likely, remind yourself it is not your job to be your parent's spouse. Expecting it to be your job is a violation and abusive. You also may need to have no contact at all with this parent for a while. That's okay. Give yourself permission to do so if that's what you need.

5. *Deal with your feelings toward the same-sex parent.* Again, writing a letter can help. Deal with your anger of being abandoned by this parent and left to be the spouse for the other. There's always a deep sense of anger regarding this. It is important to differentiate this anger from the hate and contempt you feel. Generally this hate and contempt are the feelings of the opposite-sex parent which were inappropriately transferred to you. Those feelings needed to be dealt with directly between your parents. You were caught in the middle and carried feelings that were not yours to begin with. The hate and contempt keep you from feeling an attachment to the same-sex parent. Begin to let go of those feelings by acknowledging they weren't yours in the first place.

6. *Spend some time with the same-sex parent separate from your other parent.* If this parent is deceased or too abusive to be with, find someone else who can serve as a surrogate or mentor. Often a sponsor in one of your 12-Step groups can serve this function. You eventually need to let go of this parent. Having a mentor helps this process.

7. *Get involved in a support group of men or women.* Here you can talk about your process of separation and receive support. This helps break the bond from the opposite-sex parent and supports you in your growing sense of being a man or woman.

These suggestions are not linear steps but reflect aspects of the process necessary for covert incest survivors. In time as you work through these feelings and set appropriate boundaries, your feelings of love and compassion for your parent may return. You can begin to see your parents as injured adults — as children they did not get their needs met either and were likely violated as well.

Forgiving and letting go so you can get on with your life and create working relationships is hopefully where your process will take you. It is important that you not forgive too soon. If you forgive before you work this process, it isn't forgiveness at all but denial of the truth.

ON THE MATTER OF RELATIONSHIPS

What's clear by now is that covert incest survivors struggle to have a satisfying, committed love relationship. A core issue contributing to this struggle is the confusion resulting from reacting to your spouse as if he or she were still your parent. Developing an inner boundary allows you to distinguish between these two relationships. This is a necessary step to establish a working relationship for yourself. The separation process I just described goes a long way toward that end.

In fact, I recommend that you establish a sense of separateness from your parent before you make any major decisions about your relationship. Your emancipation allows you to be more available to yourself and your relationship. If you're single, you'll be more likely to choose a mate based on adult intimacy needs rather than those of the violated and abandoned inner child. If you're considering divorce or letting go of a relationship, the separation process helps make it clearer that you are leaving the right person. The following are other considerations regarding relationships for covert incest survivors:

1. Let go of your fantasies. Remember the abandoned and hurt little child inside you has likely created a rich fantasy life about love, sex and romance as a way to cover your pain. If you continue to attempt to create adult relationships out of your fantasies, you will add to your sense of abandonment and chronic feelings of dissatisfaction. Keep working toward acceptance of the reality of yourself and your partner. You stand a much better chance at establishing a workable relationship. Allow yourself to grieve the loss of your fantasies and illusions.

2. Make a full commitment to stay in your relationship if you judge it to be good for you. Separate the insatiable needs of the inner child from the realistic intimacy needs of the adult. Regrettably all the developmental needs lost to the incestuous relationship will not be met fully in any one partnership. The sooner you accept that, the less likely your victimized inner child will project demands inappropriate to adult relationships. These demands destroy relationships which might otherwise be good for you.

3. Burn your bridges. One of the patterns contributing to the ambivalence regarding commitment is to keep a couple relationship going at once or keep the "door open" with past relationships just in case you have to make a run for it. The underlying fear behind fully committing is, "I will be used and betrayed again as I was with my incestuous parent." At stake is the fear of losing your sense of self in the relationship. Additionally, you avoid deep feelings of pain and anger by keeping yourself in this pattern.

If you are going to resolve your ambivalence regarding commitment, you need to burn your bridges by letting go of relationships (which may mean *no contact*) that are designed to keep you on the run. You also need to grieve the loss of these relationships. Remember, you deserve a healthy and intimate love relationship with one person. And you are capable of one. But you have to let go of old self-destructive behavior patterns before you can be open to intimacy.

4. Set boundaries and make your personal needs a priority in your relationship. The fear of losing yourself in a relationship is usually founded in truth. The incestuous relationship teaches you to sacrifice your needs for the love of your partner. Though this is needed at times in all relationships, you may experience a loss of choice and do it chronically. The hope is that maybe finally your needs will be met. This doesn't work, and the seeds sown for deep resentment eventually help erode the relationship.

It's okay to do what's good for you and not be concerned with pleasing your partner all the time. Setting boundaries needs to be concrete, even though you fear it will displease your spouse. It is crucial that you begin to develop a tolerance for allowing your spouse to be angry or displeased with you. If not, you'll stay stuck in the incestuous pattern of trying to please in the hope of getting your needs met. At this juncture, it is no longer your parent betraying you — it is your own self-betrayal.

You're likely to feel guilty in these attempts. Your guilt is the result of being violated in the incestuous relationship. Allow yourself to be outraged over being burdened with so much guilt. Your sense of outrage helps you to set boundaries. Adults who grew up with functional parents who did not use them to gratify their own needs do not feel enormous guilt when they attempt to get their needs met.

5. Even after all this work, you ultimately may need to say goodbye to your relationship. Not all relationships work. You may discover at some point that it is not your parent you're attempting to leave or are dissatisfied with but your spouse. As you come into your own sense of self and gain some perspective, you may realize your relationship is not good for you. Again, your sense of guilt may be tremendous. You may want to hang on so as not to hurt the other and to avoid dealing with feelings of abandonment. It's okay to leave if this is what you need to do. This does not make you a bad person.

You may need your sense of outrage at being in another guilt-ridden bind to have the presence of mind to let go. At the same time, it is important not to act out this outrage against your spouse by blaming or attacking. Don't be a victim by thinking, "This has happened to me again and it's my spouse's fault." Take responsibility for your choices, feelings and decisions. If you don't, you will have a larger blind spot to the intimacy traps in your next relationship.

6. Watch your seductive behavior. Keep your seduction in check. You don't do yourself or anyone else any favors by engaging in behavior which results in hurt, confusion and emptiness. Remember, your pattern of seduction and abandonment is a way to experience feelings of power and

control intended to help you overcome the sense of victimization as a child. But it doesn't work. If your seduction
is part of a pattern of sexual addiction, get some help.

Seductive behavior also has the purpose of hurrying
relationships along to avoid your underlying fears and
fulfill your fantasies. The seduction greatly distorts your
sense of reality of the relationship and the person you are
involved with. Once reality comes into focus, you may
begin to withdraw because you realize you have gone too
fast and become too vulnerable or realize this is not some-
body with whom you should be vulnerable. By all means,
when beginning new relationships, go slow, stay rooted
in reality and allow the relationship to unfold as it should,
not as you would have it.

LOVING YOURSELF

One of the consequences of being victimized is feeling
objectified and used, not loved. As a result, you also relate
to yourself and others as objects to be used. You probably
struggle to love yourself, having never felt loved for who
you are. Loving yourself is an important part in your
ability to love someone else. Part of the struggle with
commitment for covert incest survivors is just this.

A committed relationship is about building and nurturing an enduring love between two people. Because you
were never nurtured by your parent, you may have difficulty receiving love and nurturance. Or, on the other hand,
you may resent giving love and consequently hold back.

Your journey of recovery needs to include learning to
develop a tolerance for self-love. You do this by making
simple statements of affirmation on a daily basis.

For example, *"I love myself unconditionally"* is a place to
start. You might try this while looking into your eyes in
the mirror. You can develop any number of statements to
affirm your feelings of self-love. You also can increase
your tolerance by doing more acts of self-nurturing such
as cooking your favorite meal, going to a favorite restau-
rant, walking, talking to friends, taking a warm bath, read-

ing a good book and so on. Do more of whatever makes you feel a greater sense of self-love, provided it isn't or doesn't become self-destructive (for example, eating disorders and sexual addictions begin as ways to nurture but become self-destructive).

Another core injury is the damage caused by never learning to trust your own intuitive sense. The covertly incestuous relationship never permitted you to know and trust in your feelings because you were so preoccupied with your parents' feelings. The inappropriate dependency inhibited you from taking personal risks crucial in developing trust in your intuition.

As a child, you needed your parent to provide a safe haven where you would be nurtured when you took personal risks of autonomy. The incestuous relationship prohibited that from occurring. Your parent needed you too much to permit you the freedom to take risks. Being robbed of the freedom of autonomy is what interferes with developing trust of your intuition. It is a crucial factor in creating ambivalence regarding commitments. Ultimately, you need to be able to trust your intuitive "gut" feeling about a relationship to know what is best for you. When you mistrust this, you may over rely on your intellect. This can distort your intuitive sense. The split between the two helps create the agony of ambivalence.

Begin teaching yourself to take risks and trust your intuitive sense. Begin with small issues and decisions — make them based on your gut feelings. Keep practicing returning to this process. Remember, it is okay to do what is right for you.

Finally, keep nurturing your abandoned inner child. No one else can do it for you. Carry a picture of yourself as a child or hold an image in your mind and look at it daily. Tell your child all the things he or she needs to hear but didn't. Reassurance. Affirmation. Encouragement. You deserve it!

BIBLIOGRAPHY

Adams, K. M. "Sexual Addiction and Covert Incest: Connecting the Family Roots of Alcoholism, Neglect and Abuse." *Focus on Chemically Dependent Families*, May/June, 1987, Pompano Beach, FL: Health Communications.

Adams, K. M. "Sex Addiction Recovery and Intimacy: The Power of Romantic Delusions." *Focus on Chemically Dependent Families*, June/July, 1988, Deerfield Beach, FL: Health Communications.

Bass, E. & Davis, L. **The Courage to Heal: A Guide for Women Survivors of Child Sexual Abuse,** 1988, New York, NY: Harper & Row.

Black, C. **It Will Never Happen to Me!** 1981, Denver, CO: M.A.C. Printing and Publications Division.

Bradshaw, J. **Bradshaw On: The Family,** 1988, Deerfield Beach, FL: Health Communications.

Bradshaw, J. **Healing The Shame That Binds You,** 1988, Deerfield Beach, FL: Health Communications.

Carnes, P. **Out of the Shadows: Understanding Sexual Addiction,** 1983, Minneapolis, MN: CompCare Publications.

Carnes, P. **Contrary to Love: Helping the Sexual Addict,** 1989, Minneapolis, MN: CompCare Publications.

Diamond, J. **Looking For Love In All The Wrong Places,** 1988, New York, NY: G.P. Putnam.

Earle, R. & Crow, G. **Lonely All the Time: Recognizing, Understanding and Overcoming Sex Addiction, for Addicts and Co-Dependents,** 1989, New York, NY: Simon & Schuster.

Friel, J. & Friel, L. **Adult Children: The Secrets of Dysfunctional Families,** 1988, Pompano Beach, FL: Health Communications.

Kasl, C. D. **Women, Sex and Addiction: A Search for Love and Power,** 1989, New York, NY: Ticknor & Fields.

Lew, M. **Victims No Longer: Men Recovering from Incest and Other Sexual Child Abuse,** 1988, New York, NY: Nevraumont.

Miller, A. **The Drama of the Gifted Child: The Search for the True Self,** 1987, New York, NY: Basic Books.

Miller, A. **For Your Own Good: Hidden Cruelty in Child-Rearing and the Roots of Violence,** 1983, New York, NY: Farrar Strauss Giroux.

Miller, A. **Thou Shalt Not be Aware: Society's Betrayal of the Child,** 1984, New York, NY: Farrar Strauss Giroux.

Norwood, R. **Women Who Love Too Much: When You Keep Wishing and Hoping He'll Change,** 1985, New York, NY: Simon & Schuster.

Nouwen, H. J. M. **Reaching Out: The Three Movements of the Spiritual Life,** 1975, New York, NY: Doubleday.

Osherson, S. **Finding Our Fathers: How a Man's Life is Shaped by his Relationship with his Father,** 1986, New York, NY: Ballantine Books.

Peck, M. S. **The Road Less Traveled: A New Psychology of Love, Traditional Values and Spiritual Growth,** 1978, New York, NY: Simon & Schuster.

Subby, Robert and Friel, John, **Co-dependency And Family Rules: A Paradoxical Dependency,** Pompano Beach, FL: Health Communications, 1984.

Trachtenburg, P. **The Casanova Complex: Compulsive Lovers & Their Women,** 1988, New York, NY: Simon & Schuster.

Wegscheider, S. **Another Chance: Hope and Health for the Alcoholic Family,** 1981, Palo Alto, CA: Science and Behavior Books.

Woititz, J. G. **Struggle for Intimacy,** 1985, Pompano Beach, FL: Health Communications.

APPENDIX

The following is a list of organizations that were mentioned in the text of the book as well as others that may be helpful to the covert incest survivor:

INCEST AND OTHER CHILD ABUSE

Adults Molested as Children United (AMACU)
P.O. Box 952
San Jose, California 95108
408-280-5055

Incest Survivors Anonymous
P.O. Box 5613
Long Beach, California 90805
213-422-1632

National Child Abuse Hotline
Childhelp USA
P.O. Box 630
Hollywood, California 90028
800-4-A-CHILD (800-422-4453)

Parents Anonymous — National Office
6733 South Sepulveda Boulevard, Suite 270
Los Angeles, California 90045
800-421-0353

Survivors of Incest Anonymous
World Service Office
P.O. Box 21817
Baltimore, Maryland 21222
301-282-3400

Survivors of Incest Gaining Health (SIGH)
20 West Adams, Suite 2015
Chicago, Illinois 60606

Victims of Incest Can Emerge Survivors (V.O.I.C.E.S.)
  in Action
P.O. Box 148309
Chicago, Illinois 60614
312-327-1500

SEX ADDICTION AND THE FAMILY

Sex Addicts Anonymous (SAA)
P.O. Box 3038
Minneapolis, Minnesota 55403
612-871-1520

Co-dependents of Sexual Addicts (COSA)
P.O. Box 14537
Minneapolis, Minnesota 55414

Sexaholics Anonymous (SA)
P.O. Box 300
Simi Valley, California 93062
818-704-9854

S-Anon
P.O. Box 5117
Sherman Oaks, California 91413
818-990-6910

Sex and Love Addicts Anonymous (SLAA)
Augustine Fellowship
P.O. Box 119
New Town Branch
Boston, Massachusetts 02258

National Association on Sex Addiction Problems
1-800-622-9494

ALCOHOLISM AND THE FAMILY

Alcoholics Anonymous World Services (AA)
P.O. Box 459, Grand Central Station
New York, New York 10163
212-686-1100

Alcoholics Anonymous — General Services Office (AA)
468 Park Avenue South
New York, New York 10016
212-686-1100

Al-Anon Family Group Headquarters
1372 Broadway (at 38th Street)
7th Floor
New York, New York 10018
800-245-4656
212-302-7240 (in New York area)

National Association for Children of Alcoholics (NACOA)
31706 Coast Highway
South Laguna, California 92677
714-499-3889

Children of Alcoholics Foundation
200 Park Avenue
31st Floor
New York, New York 10166
212-949-1404

DRUG ADDICTION

Cocaine Anonymous — National Office
P.O. Box 1367
Culver City, California 90232
213-559-5833

Narcotics Anonymous — World Services Office (NA)
P.O. Box 9999
Van Nuys, California 91409
818-780-3951

National Cocaine Abuse Hotline
800-COCAINE (800-262-2463)

EATING DISORDERS

American Anorexia/Bulimia Association, Inc.
133 Cedar Lane
Teaneck, New Jersey 07666
201-836-1800

Overeaters Anonymous — National Office
4025 Spencer Street, Suite 203
Torrance, California 90504
213-542-8363

FOR ADDITIONAL SUPPORT GROUPS

National Self-Help Clearinghouse
33 West 42nd Street
New York, New York 10036
212-840-1259

Obsessive Compulsive Anonymous
P.O. Box 215
New Hyde Park, New York 11040
(516) 741-4901

Phobics Anonymous
P.O. Box 1180
Palm Springs, California 92263